Alberta Politics Uncovered

TAKING BACK OUR PROVINCE

Mark Lisac

NEWEST PRESS

Library and Archives Canada Cataloguing in Publication
Lisac, Mark, 1947-
Alberta politics uncovered : taking back our province / Mark Lisac.

ISBN 1-896300-91-X

1. Alberta-Politics and government-1971-   . I. Title.

JL336.L58 2004   320.9'7123   C2004-905290-X

Board editors: Douglas Barbour and Michael Penny
Cover and interior design: Ruth Linka
Front cover image: Kyle Riva, www.kylerivaphotography.com
Back cover image: Chris Stackhouse, www.chrisstackhouse.com
Graph on page 36: Reproduced with permission from: Alberta's Reserves 2003 and Supply/Demand Outlook 2004-2013 (Alberta Energy and Utilities Board, 2004)
Author photo: Maren Lisac

NeWest Press acknowledges the support of the Canada Council for the Arts and the Alberta Foundation for the Arts, and the Edmonton Arts Council for our publishing program. We also acknowledge the financial support of the Government of Canada through the Book Publishing Industry Development Program (BPIDP) for our publishing activities.

NeWest Press
201–8540–109 Street
Edmonton, Alberta T6G 1E6
(780) 432-9427
www.newestpress.com

1 2 3 4 5 07 06 05 04

PRINTED AND BOUND IN CANADA

For Mel, Eva, Ida and Kris – real Alberta pioneers

Table of Contents

Western alienation has for many years been a tried and true political tool in Alberta. By early 2004, there were signs its appeal was fading. Premier Ralph Klein attacked the federal government over control of health policy. The general public response was summed up in this editorial cartoon by Malcolm Mayes in February 2004.

PREFACE

Why does Alberta produce exceptional artists and hockey players, and lousy politics?

Why does Alberta produce a lot of words about Senate reform, then watch as provinces like British Columbia and New Brunswick carry the ball on real political reforms such as switching to a voting system based on proportional representation?

Why did Stockwell Day, the short-lived leader of the Alliance party, get sold to the rest of Canada as a hot political leader and then get dumped like a cold, day-old potato?

Why does a province that complains about a "democratic deficit" in Ottawa accept the operation of a virtual one-party state at home?

Why do the same people who are quick to condemn scandal and waste in the federal government ignore scandal and waste in the Alberta governement?

Why did what looked like a successful reconstruction of government in Alberta in the 1990s inspire few imitations and run aground when it was copied in British Columbia ten years later?

Why does a supposedly bold and self-confident province ricochet between self-pity and self-congratulation?

Why does a province awash in money live in dread that someone will take it, or that the flow of money will dry up?

Because . . .

POOR LITTLE RICH KID

Alberta is a place soaked in self-deception.

If Canadians in other provinces are mystified by what makes this place tick, by the problem of how a province full of material riches can be so wracked by crankiness and fear, it's because people in Alberta don't know themselves. They have become accustomed to living with what is not real.

Alberta, as it exists in the public consciousness, is a façade—a false front like the two-storey walls standing in front of one-storey buildings in countless western movies and real western towns. Its false images of itself are reproduced across the country. Its political stagnation infects all Canadians. Irrelevancies pass for events of importance here and misunderstanding prevents useful change.

The biggest deception of all is western alienation. This is one of those big-sounding phrases that people throw around when they want to sound like they know a lot. It's a handy tool for politicians trying to juice up their own reputations and the reach of their power. It's an all-purpose headline for journalists.

You know why no one can come to grips with "western alienation?" Because, no one is supposed to come to grips with it. You never see it fully defined because to define western alienation would make it real. If it were real, something could be done about it. Better to leave it floating just out of reach—a combination of half-remembered history, a handful of genuine grievances, and shrewd current ambitions. That way it can exist forever. A lot of people would no more want to get rid of it than a self-pitying alcoholic would want to lose an excuse for drinking.

The real western alienation is not a region's alienation from the rest of the country. It begins in Alberta. It is the province's alienation from itself.

Living Myths

Here is a place full of young, confident, hard-working people whose leaders and image makers cast them as the downtrodden galley slaves of Confederation—and repeat the story so often that some of their listeners believe them.

Here is a province that calls insistently for changes in Canada's political system while blandly ignoring its own descent into a one-party state with a virtually obsolete legislature and an increasingly apathetic electorate.

The government says just about everything can be run better by itself than by federal authorities, but it refuses to make decision making more local by expanding the taxation power or jurisdiction of municipalities. And, it routinely ignores Alberta residents who are not at all sure that the province ought to have all the powers it wants from Ottawa.

The province urges the vision of a diverse Canada but unsubtly tries to convince the rest of the country that Alberta itself is a monolithic place with no differences of note.

The myths of Alberta's self-image tend to centre on the fourth- or fifth-generation Albertan who's a farmer, a cowboy, an oil executive, or a roughneck. The reality is a construction worker, a transplanted Newfoundlander handling machinery at an industrial oil sands operation, a nurse or teacher, or a city dweller who usually comes here from another province or another country and probably works in an urban-based service industry. For every rodeo champion or nationally recognized business executive, there's a nationally recognized homosexual artist, but you won't find that in much of the local self-description.

The myths depend on standard and now hackneyed stereotypes—such as the "maverick" and the self-sufficient entrepreneur. In reality, Alberta is a highly conformist society in which complaints about the federal government or Eastern (actually Central) Canada make up the only accepted displays of opposition to authority. And the reality of the self-sufficient business owner—and there are many bright and successful ones—is compromised by the equal reality of agricultural and resource-extracting industries that depend heavily on government regulation, government subsidy, government-provided infrastructure, and government financial aid during periods of low prices or other disasters.

Here is a place where much, although not all, of the true alienation centres on rural fears of lost livelihood and a lost way of life. Instead of dealing with those fears directly, people and politicians try to maintain an ultimately impossible rural control of politics—either through a western-based federal party or through a provincial government whose power rests on the supremacy of a single political party.

Alberta is a place where it is fashionable to decry the channels of influence that run through Ottawa while ignoring the construction of an empire of patronage at home.

Alberta is a province that wants to change the country but refuses to change itself, or even to take a clear look at what it is really like.

Why This Matters

In the fall of 2003, the weekly *Drumheller Mail,* in southern Alberta, printed two stories about fatal car accidents. One of them told about a local man going off the highway near Lethbridge and dying in a fiery rollover that killed him, his brother, and a cousin. A few weeks earlier, a teenage girl and a middle-aged man died in a head-on collision just before midnight on an empty highway. There was no sign of alcohol or any other explanation.

For the families involved, each of these tragedies was unique and extracted deep pain. Yet the nature of the tragedies was not unique at all. Inexplicable highway deaths, especially of young people, fill rural Alberta with broken hearts and grave markers every year. Dozens die annually, often in rollovers or in collisions at remote intersections. Police and safety officials know that these deaths are linked to rural Albertans' high disregard for the use of seat belts and for the seriousness of stop signs.

You could easily build a political campaign around trying to prevent these losses. Safety campaigns work. France mobilized its population in 2002 to change one of Europe's deadliest road environments. In 2003, the number of road deaths in France fell by about 1,500 from the preceding year—20 per cent.

You could keep people alive in Alberta who are otherwise going to die. You could get them to agree that wearing a seat belt is not an assault on personal liberties. You might be able to persuade them that driving to beer-soaked bush parties is not part of a course required to graduate from high school.

If you did, scores of lives would be saved each year and hundreds more would be happier. Violent death on empty highways blights Alberta in ways that can hardly be imagined. It causes loss in proportions that politics can never begin to match. None of the federal policies and none of the real or imagined slights against the West that people complain about has done nearly as much damage.

The same edition of the weekly *Drumheller Mail* that carried stories about both collisions, accidents that claimed five lives, also printed a report of the latest political stirring in rural Alberta. Former magazine publisher Link Byfield and Alberta First party leader Bruce Stubbs had spoken at a dinner in town a few days earlier. They attracted about sixty people who paid twenty-five dollars each to hear the latest prescription for making Alberta a happier place. Alberta First had a staunch limited-government platform packed with ideas for citizen control. But the evening's presentation dwelt on what were becoming known as the ideas for building a "firewall" between Alberta and the federal government: create a separate Alberta pension plan to replace the Canada Pension Plan for everyone living in the province; create a provincial police force; and create a separate system for collecting personal income tax.

People die every month on Alberta's grim roads. With tragedy all around, Alberta politicians usually turn their eyes instead to other affairs. In mid-2004, the provincial government announced a few initiatives to act against drunk drivers and moved toward graduated licensing of beginning drivers. These measures were laudable exceptions. They never carried the imprint of the premier and his collected cabinet ministers, who had the most power to generate a new way of thinking in the province. Alberta is usually distracted from the business of improving everyday lives. It pursues wispy fears and dreams instead.

In the early 1980s, when Pierre Trudeau's push for a new constitution was upsetting both provincial leaders and a lot of ordinary people, a brief current of fear rushed through some of the population, transmitted by the more sensationalist Alberta-first media. Trudeau was said to be hatching a secret plot to turn the Bowden penitentiary just south of Red Deer into a civilian internment camp. Who would be locked up there? Why, first of all, the defiant patriots who were most aware of the scheme, they were sure the prime minister had to crush civil rights.

A virtually endless list of such oddities clogs perceptions of Alberta. Other provinces may have peculiarities. Only Alberta celebrates them and converts them into mascots of provincial identity.

These peculiarities spring from genuine roots, but they do a great disservice to both the province and the country.

A cranky fringe politician is guaranteed to garner more national attention than a high-school student killed in a rollover on a lonely secondary highway or a single mother coping with bills and taking a course in a community college to get ahead.

Picturing Alberta as the home of prickly outcasts leaves other Canadians uncertain about what really goes on here. Reaching understanding on political and cultural matters becomes more difficult in the face of that information gap.

But, the failure to understand what is really happening infects the province itself. The province is absorbed in its own myths. It is far too easy in Alberta to propose bad ideas or to ignore what most people here really want.

The reasons go far beyond the dominance of a single political party and the erosion of civil institutions capable of producing alternatives. Much of public life here is focused on the inessentials. When marginal ideas and people consume a huge amount of public discussion, it becomes more difficult to get anyone to talk about the things that really matter to most people's everyday lives.

This habit has become so deeply ingrained that you cannot always tell when people are being serious and when they are using a handy tactic that has worked well in the past.

A typical example occurred in the spring of 2004 during talks on the creation of a national securities regulator. Uniquely among major industrial countries, Canada was hobbling along with a system of separate securities regulation in each of the ten provinces and three territories. Businesses were issuing a broad and increasingly urgent call for creation of a single national regulatory body. In December 2003, a review committee reported to the federal minister of finance that it was time to create a national regulator.

The committee wrote, "There was a time when Canadian businesses seeking to raise capital were primarily located in the same region as the investors who bought their securities . . . Those days are gone. Driven by the appearance of new technologies, deregulation, declining trade barriers, and the emergence of new competitors and new financial products, capital markets that were once local are now national and international. Other countries have responded to these fundamental changes by reforming their regulatory structures to improve their international competitiveness. Canada must keep pace with these changes. Today Canada is the only major industrialized country without a national securities regulator."

The committee's recommendation for a national regulator had the backing of five of the six biggest Canadian banks; the Canadian Council of Chief Executives, representing the corporate leadership of more than 150 of Canada's leading enterprises; the Small Investor Protection Association; and other major voices. They all wanted better enforcement, lower costs, greater transparency, and simpler requirements for business start-ups.

You could hardly write a situation more in line with the official beliefs that superficially had guided the Alberta government through the preceding decade. Support from business, elimination of red tape and its associated costs, adoption of faster technology, adaptation to a globalized, information-based economy—these were some of the principal guideposts in place since 1993. Alberta should have been one of the first provinces to back the creation of a national securities regulator.

Instead, provincial Revenue Minister Greg Melchin travelled east and delivered a speech to the Economic Club of Toronto on March 30, 2004, explaining why he was leading a steering group of provincial ministers fighting the proposal. Many small companies still preferred to deal with a provincial regulator, he said. Besides, while change was needed, it was too much to expect provinces to go along with change in one fell swoop. Only Ontario supported the creation of a new national body.

And then came the clincher. If none of the other arguments worked, there was this: "How can you ask western provinces to cede authority to the federal government? Even though it is two decades later, the National Energy Program is a very, very sore spot in Alberta."

As arguments go, the NEP was a particularly out-of-place red herring. The federal government had full constitutional authority over capital markets. The NEP had disappeared in the mid-1980s, to be replaced by nearly two decades of increasing federal-provincial co-operation in the development of Alberta's oil and gas industry. The recommendation for a national securities regulator was aimed at making business easier and cheaper to conduct in every province, including Alberta.

Still, Alberta led other provinces in objecting. The federal government decided not to impose a new national regulator. The failure to act continued the costs and inefficiencies clearly pointed out by the review committee. It had spillover effects, too. One investment analyst cited the lack of a national regulator as a possible reason for years of delay in improving the rules governing the operation of mutual funds in Canada.

Melchin's Toronto speech contradicted basic Alberta policy directions but followed the province's deeply entrenched political instincts. The Alberta government generally resisted big change coming from other sources while trying to impose big changes of its own devising.

The habit of the province trying to go its own way had a long heritage. Alberta, under Social Credit governments in the 1960s, was the last province to accept medicare. Premier Peter Lougheed's time in office from 1971 to 1985 saw a history often built around saying no to the federal government.

Sometimes the opposition grew out of sound reasoning. By the 1990s, it was becoming a self-perpetuating habit, a simple determination to be ornery.

The cult of marginality was being spread by writers who found it an appealing product. They produced works based on the notion of Alberta as a province full of "mavericks."

The purest political expression of these notions came from provincial Finance Minister Pat Nelson in the opening paragraphs of her annual budget speech on March 19, 2002, part of which she acknowledged was adapted from a recently published history: "Alberta is a place like no other. We are an incorrigible lot, fiercely proud, compassionate beyond words. We deliberately face into the wind every chance we get. . . .

"Throughout our history of ups and downs, booms and busts, Albertans have shown an uncanny ability to stare down the worst possible adversity. When the storms of challenge and change gust through our province, we do not turn our backs nor search for cover to hide behind. We face directly into the wind. We tackle our problems head-on. We make the right decisions, and we move on, deliberately, decisively, and with our eyes firmly fixed on building a better future for our province."

As an accurate description of life in Alberta, this had problems as well as strengths. But Nelson's speech vividly set out a core part of the province's operating myths.

What it did not acknowledge was that the myth covered up two different realities. The price of being the maverick province that insisted on going its own way in Confederation was a vicious conformity inside Alberta's own borders. And the maverick myth—Nelson's image of facing directly into the wind conjured up what might more accurately be called the buffalo myth—was often just the psychological tool to justify a refusal to accept the costs of co-operation.

The real point of Melchin and the securities regulation story is failure of leadership. Here was an Alberta cabinet minister using the standard Alberta images of the maverick mindset (we'll find a better way) and of perpetual victimhood (remember the NEP) to put off action that even he admitted was necessary. The status quo on securities regulation was not acceptable, he said. But Alberta was not leading the way to a better future. It was leading the multiprovincial effort at foot-dragging. The reasons had nothing to do with finding the best solution to a problem. They had to do with keeping control of power for the sake of power.

That is why Alberta's self-deceptions matter to Canadians everywhere. A vigorous and ambitious part of the country often fails to live up to its own self-image. The costs pile up in Alberta and they pile up across Canada from coast to coast.

There are plenty of examples of Alberta leading the way for the country. It could lead in many other ways but chooses not to. Instead, Alberta tries to talk the rest of the country into doing things that Alberta itself will not do.

The Other Deficit

The most glaring failure to back words with action is the persistent effort to defeat federal governments and erase what has come to be called the "democratic deficit" in Ottawa. The phrase built on the fever of worry over budget deficits a decade earlier. But, Alberta's ideas for greater grassroots democracy have always suffered from a fatal drawback. The Alberta government has never demonstrated any intention to try any of them at home. The one major departure was the decision to elect a Progressive Conservative party leader in 1992 by popular vote rather than by a delegate convention—and that was a reform reserved for Conservative party members.

By 2003, you could hear frequent despair over the fact that the federal Liberals had been in power for an entire decade. The same party has been running Alberta since 1971, and its election victory in that year represented the only change of government since 1935. The premier's office is clearly the centre of power and becoming more so each year. Political choice in Alberta functions within a closed loop. Except in highly unusual circumstances such as the pivotal election of 1993—the only serious contest since 1971—everyone can be reasonably certain the governing party will win. The choice then becomes whether to vote for a voice in government or a voice in opposition. The answer is usually to vote for a voice in government. That reinforces the governing party and the choices become locked in even more tightly the next time around.

The effect gets stronger still when the governing party usually comes up with the candidates who have the most impressive backgrounds and strongest record of community service, as the Progressive Conservatives often do. And why would anyone with a solid position in the community want to run for opposition? The prize for election is putting up with casual insults in question period, being largely ignored by the media, watching government backbenchers earn much more money by virtue of being appointed to this agency or that board, and knowing that one's future employability outside politics is likely being impaired. The more attractive choice is to fight for a nomination in the governing party.

You have to be a saint to run for the ragged, perpetually debt-ridden shells that pass for opposition parties in Alberta. A saint, or someone with the character of a stubborn, defiant buffalo facing directly into a stiff wind coming off the mountains. Most people in public life here are neither. Contrary to the stereotype of the defiant individual, the province is full of people who take the easier path and join the party (literally and figuratively).

You get to laugh at this only if you live here. Anyone living outside the province has to deal with the results. What's important for the rest of Canada is why all the rules change as soon as Albertans cross into federal politics.

Misdirection

Over the years, Alberta political leaders and voters have been remarkably willing to turn against their own.

Joe Clark's nine-month tenure as prime minister featured popular sneers about his horsemanship and his willingness to live with an independent-minded wife. Alberta MPs gathered regularly in the office of Red Deer MP Gordon Towers for anti-Clark gripe sessions. While Alberta Premier Peter Lougheed and his closest ministers kept their own counsel, it was common knowledge around the Alberta legislature that many players in the provincial government supported Brian Mulroney in the leadership showdown that led to Clark's fall in 1983.

Mulroney's Progressive Conservative government was built fundamentally on a coalition of Quebec and Alberta interests. Clark retained a prime role. Don Mazankowski, who went to Ottawa after a successful career as a car dealer in Vegreville, became deputy prime minister, with genuine influence to match the title. The last vestiges of the National Energy Program were cleared away and Mulroney fought a bruising election campaign to win a mandate for a free-trade agreement with the United States, which had been one of Lougheed's most important projects, and laid the groundwork for a subsequent Alberta export boom. Alberta reached a peak of influence that seemed beyond its dreams seven or eight years earlier. But, Mulroney's term as prime minister was only three years old when new western politicians established the Reform party.

Reform's slogan was "The West Wants In." The West already was in. Some western Canadians had been in the circle of federal power all along. Something funny happened, though, every time. They were always the wrong westerners as far as some people in Alberta were concerned. They made what many people in Alberta thought were mistakes. Or, they were not "in" deep enough. They still had to make occasional compromises. They had power, but they had to share power.

"The West Wants In" was presumed to be a rallying cry for western alienation and became nationally accepted as such. But, there were several versions of "the West." Some of them were fighting one another. And, some of them did not want "in" at all; what they wanted was to create a party based on exclusion, an organization that would keep others out. This goal received perfect expression in the original constitution of the Reform party, which kept out any would-be members east of Manitoba.

In Alberta, western alienation is not just spontaneous grievance. It's something that more than 3 million people have to be convinced daily that they feel. Western alienation is the scrap-yard crushing machine that is used to squash political dissent inside the province. Many Alberta voters have to struggle against the daily message—from politicians, media, and academics—that the only true lens through which to view politics is the lens of regionalism.

Late in 2003, a veteran federal civil servant named Arthur Kroeger took part in a rare interview in which he talked about Alberta and western alienation. His comments constituted one of the few clear-minded general assessments to come from any public figure.

"You can't do one thing that's going to please the West because there is no such West . . . there are many Wests," he said.

"There's almost nothing on which you can take a position that isn't going to offend someone in the West. But at least you can get a good read of western sensitivities and what might or might not be tolerable . . ."

One of the most important ways of doing that, he said, is to involve westerners in decision making. His two prime examples of how to act and how not to act were the elimination of the Crowsnest freight rates on export grain (rail freight rates that had been fixed decades earlier and not allowed to increase with inflation) and the 1980 National Energy Program.

On the freight rates: "The railroads were being bled white, losing hundreds of millions of dollars, and the Crow was putting capital investment programs at risk. The rail companies were not about to invest in a grain transportation system when they were moving loads at an 1897 freight rate. The way we did it was we invited in all of the stakeholders—the wheat pools, the cattlemen and the like—and we shared the problem with them. Some of them didn't like what we were doing but they knew that change had to come, so they helped us work out that change."

In contrast: "The National Energy Program was devised in great secrecy and was ramrodded through."

Kroeger spoke from intimate knowledge. He had been a senior government manager in a number of departments for nearly five decades, but he was as grass-roots Albertan as you can get—a native of the town Consort, deep in the parched grain and cattle country of southeastern Alberta.

"I think the biggest single complaint from people in the West is that they feel they are not taken seriously and that people in Ottawa never view things from a western lens," Kroeger said.

That's about as profound a statement about the West and Alberta as anyone is going to make. It is likely not a coincidence that it came from someone who has lived on both sides of the conceptual divide. Saying is a long way from understanding, though, and understanding is a long way from acting. Human interaction of every sort in every country would be easier if people could manage that trick of empathy.

For Alberta, Kroeger's words deliver an unexpected sting.

A lot of Alberta's problems come from always trying to view everything through a western lens, and not taking seriously anyone who does not.

Western alienation grows out of real, or at least out of historical, roots. But, it has been transformed into an artificial and mysterious edifice. It is used now to further the power of the provincial government, and to further the political agendas of ideologically driven political activists who can in no way be described as "the grassroots."

Their method consists of manipulating populist politics for anti-populist ends. Their process hinges on geographical confusion. Alberta is made to represent "the West;" Calgary, occasionally allied with some rural areas, is made to represent Alberta. One party is made to represent all the people. Yet as Kroeger said, there is no monolithic West. And if there was, Alberta would not be its embodiment.

These misunderstandings result in a political paralysis whose main victims are Albertans themselves.

THE REVOLUTION THAT WASN'T

The election of Ralph Klein as Progressive Conservative leader in December 1992 and the subsequent election of a remade government in June 1993 supposedly began an upheaval in the way governments did business in Canada, as well as reviving conservatisim. The evidence is slim.

It was never really a conservative government, you see.

Not in the sense of a government that believed in organic development by small, step-by-step change. Not in the sense of a government whose members practised any self-restraint beyond what was needed politically. Not in the sense that it believed local or community organizations were a repository of common sense and could be trusted with money and a portion of power. Not in the sense that it ever truly gave up control of very much that it allegedly turned over to the private sector. Not in the sense that its financial policies were clear, consistent, and influenced by the need for efficient public service. Not in the sense that it really believed in "small government" at all.

The New World

An old French aphorism says the more things change, the more they remain the same. Alberta is a more aggressive place. If you want to understand what has happened here since 1992 you have to go back to an old Italian writer who wrote a novel about a political revolution around the theme: "If we want everything to stay the same, everything must change."

Ralph Klein never wanted to change the world. That kind of thinking was more to the taste of a handful of his cabinet ministers like Jim Dinning and Steve West.

Dinning was his first provincial treasurer, the overseer of the big budget cuts from 1993 to 1996. He was an ideas guy who liked talking to other people with bright ideas, usually about how to restructure an organization or a way of doing things. He came from a prominent Calgary family and had a master's degree in public administration from Queen's University. The social rank and the academic achievement made him a rarity in Klein's early cabinets. With his toothy smile and enthusiastic greetings, he could give off a vaguely Atlantic Coast prep-school aura. Yet, he wasn't a dilettante. When the province began remaking the health and education system in the late 1980s, Dinning was there, offering new directions, and making sure his colleagues heard from people he thought had interesting things to say. He may have had a larger impact than people realized. Archival evidence suggests the landmark Rainbow commission on health care in the late 1980s may have started with a suggestion from Dinning to Premier Don Getty, who backed him over objections from other cabinet ministers.

Steve West pulled the government in somewhat opposite directions. He was more a destroyer than a builder. He was a veterinarian from southwestern Ontario who moved to Alberta and liked what he found. His early career in the legislature saw him involved in a few scrapes while out drinking with Klein. He ended up salvaging his cabinet job by publicly pledging in the legislature to give up alcohol. A biography of Klein described him as a "holy terror" in the late 1980s and said, "Regulars recall how he'd throw a drink in someone's face on the flimsiest of pretexts. It could be their long hair or just a look he didn't like." After Klein took over, West started a second stage in his career by routinely gutting his departments and dumping deputy ministers. His vaguely skeletal appearance and his penchant for slashing the public payroll—all on the theory that private enterprise could always do everything better than government could—earned him the nickname Dr. Death.

Klein was more of a manager. He found getting into scraps with people irresistible, but he generally picked his targets among people he disliked or did not have to work with. His idea of how to run a government was to make problems go away. Dinning and a group of senior civil servants, fired up by new management literature built around concepts such as "re-engineering," were more attracted by the theory that good leaders always find problems. They liked the catchphrase: "If it ain't broke, break it." Klein didn't think in those terms, but he had few ideas of his own; he was susceptible to political colleagues he trusted and to business executives who made him feel accepted.

By 1992 the Alberta government's problems were mounting up. Klein had to deliver big changes if he and the Progressive Conservative party expected to hang on to power. Anyone with a bright idea saw the new government provided an opening.

And so, a lot of experiments got started that voters had not asked for. The big change of direction stopped in late 1996, just before the election the following spring. But by then, the health system had been shaken up, and the legislative wheels had been set in motion for deregulation of Alberta's natural gas and electricity markets. Both of the latter got underway with amazingly little debate.

The other provinces had a chance to buy in but didn't. Saskatchewan got to a balanced budget first and had a tougher job of getting there. The other provinces looked at Alberta's experience with initiatives like liquor store privatization, a flat-rate income tax, and electrical deregulation, and backed off. Klein himself never tried for national politics.

It was a lot like the new Soviet Union after 1917. Or like Alberta in 1938, when Bible Bill Aberhart crossed the border to campaign for Social Credit candidates in Saskatchewan and watched them stagger to two seats and 16 per cent of the vote. The revolutionaries looked around in amazement. How come the revolution didn't spread?

What's in a Name?

The phrase "the Klein Revolution" had a certain multi-layered appeal. It was partly a tool to get people to realize that big changes were coming. During the political turmoil in 1992, and the run-up to the election of June 1993, many people, including a surprising number of Liberal and New Democrat members of the legislature, did not believe the Conservatives were going to change all that much. Adapting the better known phrase "the Reagan Revolution" was a way of calling attention to the fact the new Conservative leadership was serious.

But "the Klein Revolution" was a play on words, as well. A revolution can mean more than an upheaval. It can mean something turning in a cycle. Alberta seemed to be turning in its own familiar cycle. It was going through the bust phase of a boom-and-bust economy tied to the market for raw commodities. And, it was going through one of its periodic searches for new leadership.

If Alberta was going through a historical cycle, chances were good that what looked like massive and permanent change was going to produce familiar old effects. The easiest one to predict was an eventual restoration of pay and perks for politicians. They weren't likely to practise restraint if the economy turned around, and they didn't. Government members in the legislature began earning extra pay through an amazing variety of appointments to various boards and committees. Cabinet ministers restored their habit of foreign travel, departing the province in geese-like flocks every October and January. The pensions that nearly sank the Conservative party in early 1993 made a comeback in disguised form. A deal quietly cooked up by a legislature committee just after the 2001 election provided enriched severance pay based on a formula of one year's pay for each four years served. The new deal was retroactive to 1989, meaning it covered the period during which MLA pensions were supposed to be obliterated. By 2004, many three-term MLAs and cabinet ministers could expect to leave politics with $300,000 to $500,000 and Klein stood to walk away from the premier's office with more than $500,000.

Nearly as predictable was the return of the public appetite for government spending.

As natural gas royalties started producing multibillion-dollar budget surpluses—gas royalties of $5.5 billion were primarily responsible for a $4 billion surplus in 2003–04—the province moved into a replay of the 1950s. Alberta historian Alvin Finkel's book *The Social Credit Phenomenon in Alberta* follows the evolution of the old Social Credit governments from their radical beginning in 1935 to the stable management era of the 1950s. During the later period, Premier Ernest Manning used money from the booming oil patch to keep people happy with new schools, hospitals, and highways. It was a simple formula , and it worked. Starting with the election-year budget of 1997, the Progressive Conservatives led by Ralph Klein veered in the same direction. In the first three years after Klein became premier, the Alberta government's total spending fell to $14.2 billion from $16.8 billion. From the fiscal year 1996–97 to 2003–04, total spending increased by more than 50 per cent—to $22 billion from $14.2 billion. The big difference between Social Credit and the Conservatives was that the government fifty years later had to deal with strong public-sector unions that soaked up some of the money.

This political evolution disappointed a relatively small number of hard-line fiscal conservatives. It was not a huge surprise. Alberta voters had never talked about government spending in ideological terms. They sometimes wanted government spending, and a lot of it. One of the most evocative rural Alberta scenes you could have found in the 1990s was a sign posted on a stretch of uninhabited prairie in southern Alberta during a provincial election. It stood next to a fence at a dusty crossroads, buffeted by a wind blowing out of the sage-green pasture behind it. A die-hard Social Crediter was running for the legislature with a simple message: "Waste Not, Want Not." There was a candidate you could vote for. Most of the local "conservative" voters did not.

What was more a surprise was the government's willingness to keep up the pretence after the initial tough decisions. Three lean years followed by several fat years somehow created a reputation of tight-fisted, gimlet-eyed management. Even the three lean years carried a misleading message. The new government worked hard to keep up the impression that its predecessors had been spend-thrifts. In fact, Premier Don Getty's governments during the late 1980s and early 1990s had led the country in holding down the growth of operating expenditures; they simply had not gone further and made the kinds of cuts required to close the gap left by the disappearance of $3 billion a year in resource revenues.

The image of sound management might have been harmless enough inside the province. Problems started when Alberta-based politicians tried to export Alberta-based policies across the country.

Alberta politics ran on the formula of high spending and low taxes. It was a sweet deal available only in a province that had billions of dollars of free revenue from oil and gas, and booming income-tax revenues based on an expanding pop-ulation full of young, working-age people in an economy powered by billions of dollars in capital investment.

That's a gift for any government. It also creates an unrealistic picture in peo-ple's minds. They get used to the notion that their politicians have created a cor-nucopia economy rather than the economy creating the politicians. They start asking why the rest of the country can't be run the same way. When Albertan ideas like a flat-rate income tax get rejected because it's tough to apply them elsewhere, that rejection gets used as more evidence that poor old Alberta isn't appreciated.

Alberta has another problem, though. A lot of the supposedly sharp public management just doesn't exist. Neither does the supposed preference for small government. The Klein Revolution ended with a lot of people fooling themselves.

Are You Calling Me a Liar?

More than eleven years into his time as premier, Ralph Klein was getting visibly disengaged from his job. He still snapped at reporters from time to time, threw casual insults across the floor at opposition members, and skipped appearing in the legislature for days on end with dismissive statements that he wasn't missing much. None of this made much immediate difference to his reputation. Being imperious was, in fact, firmly in the Alberta tradition. Back in the 1930s, Premier William Aberhart did not deign to make a speech in the legislature until three and a half years after he was first elected.

Klein ran into trouble in May 2004, however. He appeared before the legislature public accounts committee for the first time in years, a conspicuously large retinue in tow. There he refused Liberal MLA Laurie Blakeman's request for a receipt to back up claims that the Conservative party had paid some of his expenses during a golf trip to the Halifax area. Television broadcasts were saturated the next few days with the sight of a raspy-voiced premier repeatedly demanding of Blakeman: "Are you calling me a liar?" He finally produced a piece of paper that he had had with him all along.

The episode led to what had become a sleepily familiar exchange in letters to editors and talk-show comments. Get off Ralph's back, his supporters said. Craig Elliott, a columnist in a weekly Edmonton arts paper wrote, "Who called him a liar? It's 'Total Freakin' Spaz' that everybody's calling him, because no one who isn't a total freakin' spaz behaves that way."

Another day at the office. Except it wasn't like most other days. This little uproar took place while the country was locked into a much bigger uproar over the miserable accounting practices that led to what was being called "the sponsorship scandal" in Ottawa. The Ottawa scandal instantly scrambled whatever goodwill new Prime Minister Paul Martin had managed to build up in Alberta. Alberta MPs on the House of Commons public accounts committee were grilling witnesses in public hearings about the lack of a paper trail on advertising expenses. But here was the Alberta premier loudly and irritably claiming it was off-limits for a member of an Alberta public accounts committee to ask him to produce a receipt.

The small moment rang out like a gong. It symbolized the province's tendency to accept without comment things that stirred up major controversy in Ottawa. The self-deception ran so deep in Alberta that these things were hardly noticed, even when they were laid out in public view.

The biggest burial of what would have been a public scandal anywhere else involved a business deal between West Edmonton Mall, the country's largest retail-entertainment complex, and Alberta Treasury Branches, the government-owned financial institution set up in the 1930s to provide homegrown banking services.

In 1994, the ATB granted the mall a $355 million guarantee on a loan from TD Bank and a $65 million, thirty-year, no-interest second mortgage. That transaction generated years of legal battles beginning in 1998, when ATB accused its retired top executive "and others" of accepting bribes in exchange for arranging the loans. The former executive then alleged that he had arranged the refinancing under direction from Klein and key members of Klein's cabinet. A report from the provincial auditor general made it clear the mall financing broke ATB's rules on granting credit, putting far more money at risk with one client than was allowed. It found no evidence of direct political involvement despite memos from Klein urging that Edmonton's Ghermezian family, owners of the mall, not be foreclosed on and from senior cabinet minister Ken Kowalski pressing for continued control of the mall by the Ghermezians. Suits and counter-suits were filed by many parties.

The entire case was disposed of during a twenty-minute court proceeding on December 20, 2002. An out-of-court settlement made provisions for all parties involved and bound them all to secrecy. Among the items of missing information was whether the government-owned ATB had recovered any of the $115 million it claimed to have lost in the refinancing.

Finance Minister Pat Nelson responded, "I am pleased that ATB Financial and West Edmonton Mall have resolved all of their outstanding issues." New Democrat Leader Raj Pannu said the secret ending to the affair was "an outrage . . . the most cynical of politics, the absolute worst." People around the province settled back to enjoy Christmas.

What makes something a scandal in Ottawa and a minor disturbance that can be shrugged off in Alberta? Maybe it depends on the amount of political credit a government has stored up. Perhaps it relates to a popular wish not to discredit a leader. Klein had already survived the bruising Multi-Corp affair, a business that was never thoroughly probed and got a somewhat whitewashed recounting in an authorized biography. The new government elected in 1993 had promised little more than to balance the budget without resorting to tax increases and to help create new jobs; maybe Alberta voters expect more from the federal government.

The great restructuring of 1993 was also supposed to enhance efficiency, however. That promise has often been left unfulfilled. As with the ATB-West Edmonton Mall affair, serious questions about government accounting controls have been put before the Alberta public without raising a stir.

The Energy Department lost accounting control of billions of dollars a year in natural gas royalties for a couple of years in the mid-1990s, essentially relying on gas producers to file accurate production and royalty reports. It cost at least $37 million to develop a new computer system to track royalties.

Annual reports from the provincial auditor general outlined that failure. They did not raise a ripple. One good reason for the calm is that better government ancial control would be highly inconvenient. A lot of people around Alberta would find themselves on the receiving end of questions.

The auditor's comments on the 2002–03 fiscal year included the Tax Exempt Fuel Users' Program, which provides rebates and exemptions worth about $120 million a year on fuel used off-road for commercial purposes (as in the forestry and energy industries). Fewer than one per cent of claimants had been audited. But those audits were enough to lead to the recovery of $1.9 million over two years. The auditor's office added that it could not determine the objectives of the rebate program.

The Farm Fuel Distribution Allowance gives farmers a similar exemption from Alberta's nine-cents-a-litre gasoline tax and a rebate of six cents a litre on diesel fuel. The program was supposed to be limited to fuel used in farm vehicles and is also worth about $120 million a year. About 60,000 farmers claimed exemptions in 2002–03. There were twenty audits, but that was enough to lead to the recovery of $49,000. No one was asking whether it might be worth checking on the other 99.7 per cent of claimants.

The 2001 auditor's report found that ninety-five private vocational schools providing training for the Human Resources and Employment Department had not signed contracts with the department. The schools were not being monitored as required. A year later, the Human Resources Department spent $132 million on its skills development program (SDP), $30 million of which was reimbursed by the federal government under a cost-sharing agreement. The auditor said the department "does not have adequate assurance that the 302 training providers currently delivering the SDP are meeting the terms of the program. . . . The Department does not have assurance that students are receiving adequate instruction and training and that training providers are spending the funding appropriately."

The skills development program had been part of the province's much touted welfare reforms during the post-1992 restructuring. Relations with private training schools were a murky area for a long time. Human Resources Minister Clint Dunford shed a bit of light on what had been going on for years when he told the legislature in 2004 how the program's costs were being reduced: "We're going to see within Human Resources and Employment a transition on how we look at skills because we're really not going to be training for training's sake any more, just so we get them off the welfare rolls, you know, put them in training so our numbers look better on the welfare side. Can't do that anymore. Won't do that anymore. What we're going to have to do is see the standards set higher for who qualifies for training and the kinds of training that they will actually be seeking."

The government had insisted that its welfare reforms were admired and copied elsewhere. Welfare spending dropped by hundreds of millions of dollars and that was good enough for most voters. But tucked into the reformed system were poorly examined niches of activity that may or may not have wasted scores of millions of dollars a year. It wasn't much different from the "scandal" that had shaken the federal human resources ministry under Jane Stewart. Yet the haphazard monitoring and unsigned contracts in Alberta were passed over in silence by a population willing to believe that Alberta had found the secret to efficient government.

Operating Myths

Early in 2004, the Canadian Federation of Independent Business complained about the amount of red tape laid on small business owners by the Alberta government. A federation spokeswoman said it was true the number of regulations on the provincial statute books had dropped to several hundred from about 1,400 in the preceding decade. But much of the decrease, she pointed out, reflected the simple trick of taking several related regulations and rolling them into one big one. That had been obvious from the start, for anyone who cared to look. Mostly, nobody bothered to look.

The revolution had delivered an unmistakable basic success. Budgets were balanced and the provincial debt was rapidly shrinking. But the promised switch to clear accounting? To getting government "out of the business of business?" To rational planning? To smaller government? That would have meant giving up political control, which was the last thing on this group's mind.

The signal feature of modern Alberta government budgets is that they are no firmer than a lump of modelling clay. Revenue and spending estimates routinely change by billions of dollars, or as much as 20 per cent of original estimates. The "budget" is just a rough guide and a statement of the year's plan for taxation.

Three-year plans and performance measures proliferate, then prove no more reliable than the old Soviet Union's five-year plans and the habit of bragging about the plans' statistical achievements: they are a bureaucratic product that no one really believes.

The language of financial control has partly been drained of meaning. You can look at Alberta budget documents in vain for the annual prediction of a budget surplus. What is set out is a number for an "economic cushion." It is all the more spongy because some revenue is transferred into special accounts set up for capital projects and financial reserves. Here's what you end up with in the world of what is advertised as "transparent" government accounting: numbers that change constantly; numbers that are difficult to understand even when you can get them to stop moving around; fuzzy words; rules that are bent to suit the government's whim.

The province's balanced-budget law should have been a tip off. The first version was revised in 1999 and renamed the Fiscal Responsibility Act. That version lasted seven months before the government found it inconvenient and changed it. The bill, introduced in February 1999, required that at least 75 per cent of any annual budget surplus had to go toward debt payment. By September, the cabinet decided to throw a lot of money into construction projects. What to do? Easy—just rewrite the 75-per-cent rule that they had put into law a few months earlier. A later variation of the law put a limit on how much oil and gas revenue the government could use in a given year. In 2003, the cap was set at $3.5 billion. Any extra had to go into a special reserve fund. By the next year the cap was inconvenient, and the government changed it to $4 billion.

The final joke was the decision to abandon the balanced-budget law in practice while appearing to keep it. In 2003, the province created a "sustainability fund." The purpose was to set aside some of the revenue pouring in during times of high energy prices for use if some fiscal disaster squeezed the budget in future years. This was a good idea, one of a number of good ideas the province managed to hide under a welter of evasions and grandiose claims. Economists had been warning for some years that the balanced-budget law put too tight a noose around government finances. How to get out of the problem? Put aside money from good years and spend it, if necessary, in bad years. What went unspoken was that this plan created a way of running annual budget deficits. If the province paid its bills in year X by spending money that had been put into the sustainability fund during the two years earlier, it would be running a deficit and paying the bills with its financial reserves. It turned out that deficits were okay in Alberta. Someone just had to find a fancy fig leaf with which to cover them.

What's That You Say?

The three pillars of the Klein Revolution were centralized control, privatization, and flat taxes. Budget controls could come and go. Spending cuts could come and go. But these three elements remained. You could easily miss the true transformation because there was a lot of willingness to go along with whatever the government said and the way it said things. Of the three, privatization of public functions developed the spottiest record. It was the most difficult to achieve, although the government made some of the first steps look easy.

Klein and Steve West, then the minister in charge of the liquor board, announced in the fall of 1993 that the government's liquor stores would be sold and liquor retailing transferred to private entrepreneurs. There had been no specific public debate. They said the idea had generally been kicking around in public view and that was good enough. The privatization of liquor sales took place at a superficial level. It was also an exercise in centralized control. The government kept control of taxation and set politically influenced rules about who could open stores. It tried to protect individual business owners by keeping grocery stores out of the market for five years. Then it allowed grocers in, but only if they put up separate buildings for their beer, wine, and liquor sales. In a choice of words that summed up the government's radical approach to managed capitalism, West said, "That is the free market that we have allowed."

What went missing afterward was any honest attempt by the government to add up the pros and cons of the decision. Calgary economist Greg Flanagan did a private study years afterward. He pointed out that the number of retail outlets in the province had approximately tripled under privatization and so had the number of retail jobs, with the offset that wages for retail clerks had been cut in half. The result was that overhead costs had about doubled. It used to cost something more than $400 million a year to sell beer, wine, and liquor in publicly owned stores. By 2003, it cost more than $800 million a year. The government made up the difference by freezing its share of overall revenues, leaving more on the table so that store owners could make a profit. Ron Stevens, minister in charge of the industry, said about Flanagan's study, "I can tell you that 80 per cent of Albertans are very satisfied with the way things are going and 20 per cent of Albertans don't drink." The government did not produce any other study of the effects of liquor privatization.

The privatization of highway maintenance in 1995–96, also accomplished while West was minister in charge, suffered a similar lack of accounting. West had promised a saving of $21 million a year. Had the promise been delivered? The government commissioned a handful of studies, but they were not conclusive. A separate study by researcher Lisa Prescott, published by the Parkland Institute in 2003, found too little information for a firm conclusion. There were rumours that costs had actually increased.

The lack of transparency showed up again in the centralization of various administrative functions in a new corporate service agency. West, once again the minister involved, promised the reorganization would cut relevant costs by 20 per cent. The provincial auditor general looked at the service agency's record for the 2001–02 fiscal year. His report said, "The Centre was expected to achieve 10 per cent gross operating savings for the year. However, it did not identify a baseline from which to gauge the 10 per cent savings, nor did it clearly define the term 'savings.'" Some of its claimed savings involved a redeployment of staff, who continued to work in other ministries.

On the plus side, the government was doing a good job of making all sorts of financial information available on the Internet, and of publishing the information faster and in more detail than ever. Exactly what the flood of numbers meant and whether anyone paid attention to them was another matter.

You Can't Scare Me, I'm Sticking to the Union

Saying the Klein Revolution's agenda was built around centralized control, privatization, and flat taxes missed one other important element, however. The truly unexpected development was the transformation of a populist movement into an empire of patronage. At the core of the restructured ways of doing business was not wise financial policy, but the maintenance of an oligarchic grasp on power.

While many Alberta voters were applauding the early moves against public-sector unions, they missed the entrenchment of the biggest union of all—complete with bossism, perks and featherbedding. To get what you wanted you needed a union card, and that card was a Conservative party membership.

The rewards began at the top with the revival of pensions under the guise of severance pay. Government members of the legislature didn't have to wait for a payoff, however. They routinely earned extra pay ranging from about $13,000 a year to about $23,000 for sitting on dozens of committees, councils, agencies, and boards. The list included bodies such as the Youth Secretariat, the Employability Council, the Fees and Charges Monitoring Committee, the Alberta Science and Research Authority, the Francophone Secretariat, the Human Rights, Citizenship, and Multiculturalism Education Fund Advisory Committee—even the Regulatory Review Secretariat. Six MLAs earned extra pay of more than $23,000 a year for chairing committees of other government MLAs.

Next, there was the cabinet—trimmed to seventeen positions during the restructuring of 1993, expanded to 24 after the 2001 election gave Klein so many government members that he had to find prestige, pay, and influence to spread around. This featherbedding aggravated the constant reorganizations that plagued government departments, all of them making it difficult to track costs and achievements, all of them requiring the creation of new bureaucracies, new offices, and new letterhead stationery.

Steve West symbolized the contradictory impulses inside this politicians' union. He left government after the 2001 election to become an executive in a privately owned oilfield services firm. Early in 2004, he returned to Edmonton to become Klein's chief of staff. In an interview that February, he said: "I came back because it's tugging at my heartstrings to still serve the people of Alberta. When you walk away from this job, it's in you forever." Cabinet ministers from an earlier day—successful businessmen and lawyers like Hugh Planche, John Zaozirny, and Lou Hyndman—had found it easier to continue in their new lives.

It was not his first surprise. West told the Edmonton Chamber of Commerce in a speech in September 2000: "Government just has to stand back, stay in their cage where they belong." But when former premier Don Getty's office archives were released to the public, West had the distinction of being the one elected person in government who had left a note recommending a constituent for a job in the civil service. Asked about this later, he said he must have written many such notes, and it was part of an MLA's job.

These events, and others like them, let the politicians keep up with the Joneses in the private sector. Most voters weren't complaining. The freer spending expanded when necessary to pre-election handouts ranging from energy subsidies to sudden new spending in schools and hospitals. The government filled its side of an implicit bargain by waiting until the economy started surging ahead again before padding the job list at the party hiring hall.

But, working the connections had wider effects. One of the promises of 1993 had been an end to the patronage that had become something of a sore point with many voters. Several years later, it was common to read through the weekly lists of cabinet orders and spot familiar Conservative names among the appointments.

And, the Progressive Conservative party itself was raking in money. Its fundraising had a snowball effect. The more money the party raised, the more that people and organizations felt they had to be part of the game. The annual premier's dinners, in a number of cities, became a kind of political-social event. People said they went because it was the place to meet everyone who counted. Municipal officials and even some media executives bought tickets. The fact that most of the money went to support one political party seemed an afterthought, if it was thought of at all.

Whatever You Say

Listening to ordinary people was an essential hallmark of the cluster of events and attitudes that made up the Klein Revolution. The party's election slogan in 1993 had been "He Cares, He Listens." The commitment to listening answered many voters' deepest frustrations.

Both Klein's ascendancy and the charged political atmosphere of Alberta in 1992 and 1993 followed familiar patterns. A democracy spooked by political and economic crisis put its faith in a new leader. It chose a leader evidently connected with big businesses that might help the economy, but one who acted like he was one of the little guys.

Klein's reputation would last long after his personal interests evolved toward fishing at an exclusive lodge on the northern BC coast, dinners with top corporate executives, and golf at tony courses across the country. The association with the wealthy and powerful did not necessarily hurt him. A lot of people in Alberta were more suspicious of their neighbours than of predictable corporate leaders. Who knew what the couple next door might try to chisel out of the government? Several years after the Revolution, a columnist in a free Edmonton arts weekly described Klein as "the big shot he so clearly enjoys being, with planes at his disposal and side trips to fancy golf resorts, instead of just another high school dropout with a booze problem." But many voters were still inclined to describe the premier with words like "110-per-cent Albertan."

Klein led a program of phoney populism. Letting voters affect decisions directly had less appeal than letting them speak through government-organized polls and focus groups. You could not say that the government did not listen to the people. On the whole, it often did. MLAs stayed in touch with constituents. Polls and focus groups were common. Paradoxically, the one mechanism that wore down during the Klein years was the Progressive Conservative party convention. These events tended to draw 800 to 1,000 delegates instead of the 1,200 to 1,500 more common during the 1980s. They also drifted more toward becoming weekend parties than serious occasions for policy discussion. Some PC members were also getting restless about the cost of attending—as officials developed a preference for meeting in the Rocky Mountain resort towns of Banff and Jasper rather than in large population centres.

Yet, the listening reflex was selective. By the 2000s, the government with an image of speaking for everyone in the province was often remarkably out of step with public opinion.

Alberta and Quebec became the only two provinces in Canada to refuse to join the new National Health Council in 2004. A lot of people might have taken the province's position as representing the position of its people. Yet, an Ipsos–Reid poll in May 2003 showed a province whose ordinary voters were much happier with the idea than their government was. The poll asked whether people believed a National Health Council should be created. In Alberta, 79 per cent of respondents said yes, right in line with the 81-per-cent yes answer across the country.

The same thing happened with an attempt to control auto insurance rates. The government, worried by the way anger over steep increases in rates had nearly toppled the provincial Conservatives in New Brunswick, spent several months in 2003 and 2004 working up changes to the system. The review was carried out in private by Conservative members of the legislature and by government officials who met with industry representatives and related parties such as injury lawyers. The public was not directly consulted. The government began by ruling out only one alternative—creation of public auto insurance. An Environics poll done in June 2003, two weeks after public insurance was ruled out, found 59 per cent of people in the province wanted public auto insurance. The same result showed up in a poll commissioned by Sun Media in May 2004. That poll found 58 per cent of people in the province wanted public auto insurance, compared with 24 per cent who wanted to keep the existing private insurance system. Tough beans. What were people going to do? Break with the institutionalized party of the Revolution and vote for someone else?

The years of the Klein Revolution saw incursions into the jurisdictions of local authorities such as municipalities and post-secondary institutions. They saw an appetite for regulating personal behaviour with laws requiring things like the use of bicycle helmets by children and adolescents. The pursuit of parents not making required child support payments led to ever-increasing use of bureaucratic force; the tools included taking lottery winnings over $1,000, tapping retirement savings accounts, and refusing to issue licences for driving, hunting, or fishing to anyone behind on payments. By 2004, the government was considering a law allowing employers to force their staff to be tested for drug use.

Reducing government turned out essentially to mean reducing public debate. Public scrutiny was controlled, too. Access to information laws had to contend with political monitoring of all requests. Some information was locked up; during a flap over travel spending in 2004, the government simply closed the formerly open access to the travel logs of the province's fleet of four aircraft (itself hardly a symbol of small government). Legislature sittings were tightened to become among the shortest in Canada. Question period began to yield insults rather than answers; Klein often avoided answering questions directly in the legislature and provided the relevant information instead in his regular post-question period news conferences. Closure on debate of legislation began to be practised routinely—more than thirty times in the government's first two terms and frequently afterward.

Legislature debates weren't high in most voters' priorities. The populist rebellion of 1992–93 favoured reduced political discussion. Far more noticeable was a cute double shuffle in early 2002 that hit grassroots organizations around Alberta and shifted power from them to government MLAs.

By then, the government could count on raising about $1 billion a year through video lottery terminal profits and other gaming revenues. It had allowed community lottery boards to allocate $52 million of that amount to local projects. The 2002 budget ended the lottery board program. After sharp protest around the province, $30 million of lottery funding for community initiatives was restored. But now, the 88 local volunteer boards were replaced by a central government office. Government MLAs would hand out the cheques. Local initiative would be stifled by a new $75,000 cap on projects and by a requirement that grants go only to capital projects. Some community leaders made comments along the lines of this one in a letter to the *Edmonton Journal* from Treena Fenniak: "Decisions will be partisan, so he (Klein) can exclude groups that don't align themselves with conservative principles."

Then again, it was getting awfully tough in Alberta to figure out exactly what "conservative" meant.

MONEY

There's never enough money. There's always a reason to worry. It's a frame of mind that author Mavis Gallant, in a story that referred to growing up on the Prairies, wisely described as a combination of ambition, terror, and dry pride.

The Canada West Foundation does regular surveys gauging how optimistic people in each of the four western provinces are about the medium-term future of their economy and society. In 2001, 57.1 per cent of the people surveyed in Alberta thought the province would be much better off or somewhat better off in five years. The economy was stepping along quite nicely in 2001. By 2003 it was picking up even more speed, but strangely, only 37.3 per cent of people in Alberta thought the province would be better off in five years. A year later, optimism remained stable at 37.5 per cent. Optimism in BC and Saskatchewan lagged behind Alberta but improved over the same period.

The Alberta government was not as subdued. The premier appeared on television for his annual address to the province in February 2004 and said, "We will enter our second century with the best fiscal record in the country, the lowest tax burden, and a track record on eliminating debt that is unmatched in Canada."

That single-minded focus on money may have offered a clue. What does it say about a place when the main thing on its mind is money?

The Big Payoff

The numbers are gaudy, and they are almost all encouraging, at least if you happen to live here.

Alberta has about 10 per cent of Canada's population. In 2002, Statistics Canada was reporting that Alberta also had 11.32 per cent of the country's personal income. Personal income per person was $32,822 in Alberta versus $28,802 in Canada as a whole. After payments to government, disposable income in Alberta was $25,704 per person compared with $22,272 a person for all of Canada. You could use these income measures to predict when an Albertan government will find itself in political trouble. The political upheaval of the early 1990s peaked in 1992, a year in which personal disposable income in Alberta dipped to only $206 above the national average—cause for shame and panic.

By the end of 2003, average weekly wages were second only to Ontario.

Property taxes on single-family homes were among the lowest in the country, about $1,000 a year less on average than in southern Ontario. The unemployment rate was 4.8 per cent—the lowest in Canada and far below the national rate of more than 7.4 per cent. Retail sales were growing by 4.1 per cent a year compared with the national average of 3.1 per cent. Provincial tax rates were the lowest in the country. Best of all, as far as most people in Alberta were concerned, this was the only province without a provincial sales tax. Ah, but was it? If you looked closely, it appeared that freedom from a sales tax was another self-deception, nursed along by government language and a public willingness to believe.

In 2000, economists Ken McKenzie from the University of Calgary and Bev Dahlby from the University of Alberta published two papers urging creation of a provincial sales tax as "a better Alberta Advantage." It fell by the wayside, as might have been expected in a place where the lack of a sales tax has become a symbol of provincial identity. Nothing dented the resistance to a sales tax, despite the obvious interest of the government itself.

Various economists and the professional body representing the province's chartered accountants had for some time urged creation of a sales tax. They weren't alone. During the 1992 leadership campaign, Klein's response to a questionnaire on economic policy from the Canadian Manufacturers' Association raised the possibility of creating a provincial sales tax. In 1994, a provincial tax reform commission said that shifting from income tax to a sales tax could encourage more economic growth. Stockwell Day, preparing to deliver his last budget speech as provincial treasurer in 2000, mused about having a public debate within a few years on creating a sales tax in exchange for eliminating provincial income tax. He said the trade-off might be ready for public airing in about 2005: "Albertans may be open to that discussion." What better 100th birthday present on top of the arithmetical elimination of the province's debt? By 2004, various sources were floating suggestions for a municipal sales tax, which had the virtue of leaving municipalities to take the political blame.

There's just one little problem. Alberta already has sales taxes. That was one of the major points raised by McKenzie and Dahlby. McKenzie pointed out the province had "commodity taxes" charged on retail sales of items including tobacco, gasoline, and hotel room stays. Alberta's commodity tax levels came out at 41 per cent of the average for all other provinces. There were other kinds of taxes disguised as fees. Alberta already charged a recycling fee on every tire sold in the province. By

2004, the environment minister was proposing a hefty recycling fee on all consumer electronic equipment. The province was also expecting to rake in $165 million in 2004–05 from taxes on insurance premiums, which it called "insurance tax." Alberta has all sorts of taxes on retail sales. There are more all the time. They are worth more than $1 billion a year. They just aren't called sales taxes.

The illusion was enhanced by the turn to service fees, which amount to a form of flat-rate sales tax on all sorts of things sold to ordinary citizens by a government that been turning itself into a bigger and bigger business. The move toward fees began before the Klein era but ramped up in earnest with dozens of new charges in 1994. It gained ground yearly. Many of the fees applied to activity that the province required. For example, the province decided to mandate continuing education for insurance agents. Then in 2004, it began levying $250 fees on the providers of accredited insurance courses, and $100 fees for the approval of continuing education courses in insurance.

Municipalities, under fiscal pressure from sharply reduced provincial grants, turned mostly to property tax—but partly to tens of millions of dollars in "franchise fees" tacked on to their utility bills. Starting in the early 1990s, over a period of ten years, university tuition fees rose 160 per cent.

Then, there was the biggest user fee of all—medicare premiums, which rose to $1,056 a year for families in 2004 from $552 a year in 1990. Actually, the premiums were a form of tax. Economists pointed out they shared no characteristics with real insurance premiums: they were not risk-rated; they were not tied into an investment pool; they were set at rates defined solely by political convenience; they were put into the province's general revenues; and they were hidden wherever possible. Alberta budget documents never admitted the true rate of medicare premiums. The interprovincial tax comparison tables always showed the premiums at 75 per cent of their actual rate; the official theory was that a discount was fair because some employers paid part or all of the premiums for their employees.

Medicare premiums were also the most regressive, haphazardly collected, rapidly rising, and inefficient tax the government collected. Officials did not like to release numbers routinely, but even by 1999, signs of trouble were showing up. The province was spending about $11 million a year to collect premiums separately from other taxes. Every year it sent about 80,000 accounts to collection agencies, which charged $4.5 million for their services. Every year about $20 million to $30 million in premiums were written off as uncollectible. Every year some people had to pay the premiums out of their own pockets while others had premiums partially or fully paid by employers (with the benefit subject to income tax).

The rising premiums were a way of focusing attention on health costs. They also gave the government an effective way to entrench its policy of flat taxes. Hundreds of thousands of people on low incomes received a full or partial subsidy on their premiums. But if you earned $42,000 a year you paid the same premium as someone earning $420,000—not just a flat-rate tax, which raises more money as income goes up, but an unabashed flat tax. The difference: at $42,000 a year, the premium was a tax levied at a rate of 2.5 per cent of gross income; at $420,000, the tax rate was 0.25 per cent of gross income.

The continual slide toward heavier medicare premiums took a system already made unique in Canada by the introduction of a provincial flat-rate income tax in 2001 and made it more regressive. That switch was all right with a lot of people. It was made palatable by a cut of more than $1 billion in income taxes. It benefited some people much more than others. But complaining that some people had a better deal was unseemly, unless the others meant people in other provinces. That's one of the benefits of "western alienation" for alienation's practitioners. It keeps political debate in Alberta focused on regional equity rather than on individual equity.

A Flat Debate

The notion of a flat-rate income tax first surfaced seriously in the 1994 report on taxation. Few people seemed to pay attention. Here was another exhibit in self-deception. A province continually and loudly demanding a say in federal affairs—a province that had made opposition to the GST a major reason for turning against Brian Mulroney's Conservative government—let one of the biggest changes ever imposed in its tax system go by without public debate.

Stranger yet, the move to a flat-rate tax was a triumph of anti-populist politics. The province put its trust in a leader because he looked ordinary. Letters to newspapers and calls to radio talk shows frequently featured complaints about "elites" and academics. Yet, a tax system devised in secrecy by a tax review committee made up of academics, corporate executives, and senior civil servants, became law without a hitch.

The two big selling points were simplicity and overall lower taxes. The "simpler" system saw every Alberta taxpayer suddenly having to fill out two tax calculations rather than one. The old system, used by every other province except Quebec, had required simply calculating provincial tax as a percentage of federal tax owing. One other hoped-for benefit was slow showing up. The tax review committee thought Alberta would lead the way for the rest of the country. Its report, in October 1998, said a flat-rate provincial income tax in Alberta would help persuade other provinces and the federal government to move to a similar system. There was no stampede in that direction, just as there had been no stampede to copy other Alberta initiatives. One reason was probably that only Alberta could afford the twin fallouts that moving to a flat-rate system required: massive revenue losses, and a hosing for middle-income earners who did not gain nearly as much as higher-income earners, and who stood to lose hundreds of dollars a year if the tax rate went up by even half a percentage point.

A separate calculation for provincial income tax caused more complications than merely requiring everyone to fill out a second tax form. A single-rate income tax could severely hurt people at the bottom end of the income scale. The only way around that was to increase the basic personal exemption. When the federal government reduced its middle-income tax rate, the province had to trim even more. Its proposed 11-per-cent flat tax had to drop to 10.5 per cent and then to 10 per cent; if not, middle-income earners in Alberta would have ended up paying more than middle-income earners in some other provinces. The switch to a flat-rate income tax was initially supposed to cost the government an estimated $800 million in reduced revenues. After the federal tax cut, fixing the numbers cost another $460 million. If the federal government adopted a flat-rate income tax that also protected lower-income earners, it would see a revenue drop of more than $10 billion a year, which it can't afford.

That was the easy part to understand. The government was less forthcoming about some trickier matters. Several months after the release of the tax committee report in 1998, Treasury Department working papers on the tax change were released in response to a request under Alberta's access to information law. They showed the costly mathematics of keeping everyone happy while still catering to special interests.

The switch to a flat-rate tax was going to save $594 a year for a two-income family making $60,000 a year and raising two children. The same kind of family earning $100,000 was going to benefit by $836 a year, with tax savings rising rapidly beyond that point. A single person earning $100,000 a year was going to save $1,541 a year. That much was admitted in the province's 2001 budget documents.

The working papers showed the benefit could have been spread much more evenly if the province had moved to a two-rate system—say, a basic rate of 10 per cent on the first $59,000 earned and a rate of 12 per cent on any income beyond that level. The benefits would have been spread more evenly and the province would have avoided having to provide exemptions that cost it hundreds of millions of dollars.

The benefits were going to be concentrated geographically as well. Calgary was clearly the centre of wealth in Alberta, as well as the centre of Conservative support. The 2001 federal census showed a clear separation of Calgary from Edmonton and from the rest of the province. Income statistics showed 20.4 per cent of Calgary households earning $100,000 a year and over in the year 2000, compared with 12.6 per cent in Edmonton, and 16.2 per cent in Alberta as a whole. Average annual household income was $72,663 in Calgary and $57,360 in Edmonton. Furthermore, the geographic concentration of income had been growing. The 1996 statistics had shown a much tighter grouping of incomes of $100,000 a year or more—11.5 per cent of households in Calgary, 8.6 per cent of households in Alberta, and 6.7 per cent of households in Edmonton.

There was a nasty and poorly explained twist in the calculations, too. The spousal exemption for provincial taxes was raised by several thousand dollars to help couples earning only one income. No one explained why this was a priority. One-income families gained a tax saving of several hundred dollars a year. Their gain made less money available for others, and made a hash of other provincial policies. Treasury officials had observed that one-earner couples already had more discretionary income than working couples paying for child care. That information was swept aside. The single-income couples were going to become even better off.

More than that, children were not a factor for nearly half of the single-income families. Census data indicated that about 40 per cent of single-income couples in Alberta did not have children under eighteen living at home. For them, the big new tax bonus was not a help in raising a family; it was more likely a help in paying for a winter break in Mexico. Married couples with children, on the other hand, were finding it increasingly tough to make ends meet unless both of them worked. About two-thirds of families with children in Alberta had both parents working. They were not likely to give up the second income just to gain several hundred dollars a year in a new tax break.

But, the spousal tax exemption was defined to include the exemption allowed to single parents (about 80 per cent of them mothers). They now had more incentive than ever to go to work and have someone else look after their children. Encouraging work was not a bad idea. Leaving more money in the hands of nearly 80,000 single parents was an unreservedly good idea (although an idea the government took care not to advertise). However, this encouragement to work ran opposite to the government's romanticized rhetoric of happy family life with stay-at-home parents—the very image that fuelled the political appeal of a higher spousal tax exemption. Not everything in Alberta is what it seems.

There was a further twist. The Treasury Department's working papers pointed out longer-term implications of a separate Alberta tax calculation that the tax review committee chose to leave out of its report. The most serious involved the ability to accommodate novel departures in other major policy areas.

"For example," the papers said, "we could . . . increase tax relief for medical expenses or tuition, introduce a non-income tested child or age tax credit or a special credit for all Albertans." This was the first hard evidence that anyone in the government was thinking of higher medical and tuition tax credits. Higher tax credits would, of course, go hand in hand with even higher tuition fees. They could also go hand in hand with medicare reforms aimed at shifting more of the cost of health care onto individuals. For that matter, new business tax credits could be devised as an alternative to the discredited old system of loans and loan guarantees. The tax committee's report recommended not going in that direction. Inevitably, within a few years, new visions of economic development started leaning in that direction anyway.

The Day the Oil Ran Out

Alberta's low tax rates are made possible by high oil and gas revenues. Why didn't the oil run out? Peter Lougheed kept saying during the nasty fight over the NEP back in 1980–81 that Alberta needed all the revenue it could get from oil because the oil was going to run out in ten years.

Well, that was conceptual. The concept was that the oil would not in fact last forever. Behind that thought was deep-seated instinct. Alberta is a place historically consumed with worry that good times always mean bad times must be just around the corner—almost a biblical judgment on excess.

In 1980, Alberta had oil reserves that would last about ten years at then-current rates of consumption. Left out of the concept was some fine print: pro-

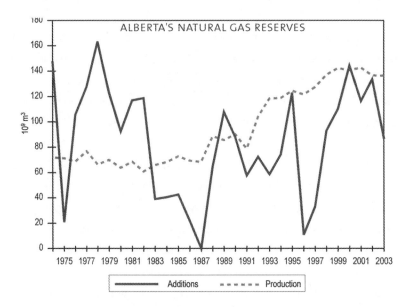

ALBERTA'S NATURAL GAS RESERVES

Legend: ———— Additions   ▪ ▪ ▪ ▪ ▪ Production

duction was always being partially replaced by new finds; the oil sands could someday yield vast new production; and, in the meantime, Alberta was really a natural gas province more than it was an oil province.

Twenty years after Lougheed's big fight with Pierre Trudeau, the province was having it both ways. Conventional energy reserves were running out, but there were big hopes that new energy resources would come on-stream. Meanwhile, the government built its financial reputation on an unsubtle strategy of ransacking available resources as fast as possible. Crucially, the huge new energy revenues did not depend solely on rising prices.

In the mid-1980s, the federal and provincial government instituted a deregulation that took limits off natural gas exports. Treasurer Dick Johnston looked at prospects for natural gas and predicted, to a Conservative convention in 1990, that energy revenues would lead to a balanced budget in about five years. Natural gas production took a noticeable jump in 1992. The Klein-era governments encouraged that expansion and pushed it to its physical limits. Production kept rising significantly every year until 1999, when it began to flatten. The key to unlocking this bonanza was a 50-per-cent increase in exports to the United States. Prices began to spike in later years, enhancing the effect of higher production, but the key was the vastly enhanced export volumes.

It was a fun ride while it lasted, especially for the politicians in charge. But, the big pools of gas had been found by the early 2000s. The wells drilled in the shallow gas pools of southern Alberta had a tendency to fall into steep production rate declines after only a year or two. There was still a lot of gas around, but the end of growth was in sight, as the province's Energy and Utilities Board began quietly pointing out. Natural gas production in the province peaked in 2001. Alberta's 100th birthday in 2005 would be celebrated during the early years of a long, inevitable decline. The "mortgage," as the political leaders liked to call government debt, would be paid off just in time.

There aren't many ways to make up this missing growth. The government hopes to see oil sands royalties kick in at a massive rate within a few years, and that seems a strong possibility. Coalbed methane production has started, but the environmental costs and potential revenue from that resource remain unclear. The price of gas could keep going up, which would sustain government revenues while draining money out of households through higher utility bills.

When people in Alberta worry about the end of the good times coming around, almost like a biblical judgment, they are not always imagining things.

Living on the Credit Card

There's rich, and then there's really rich. Alberta is sort of rich, but still has to ask how much things cost.

The $12 billion Heritage Savings Trust Fund helps calibrate where the province stands financially. The Fund is only about two-thirds the size of Harvard University's endowment fund. On the other hand, it is about the same size as the endowment fund at Yale University; that's something, at any rate.

The Fund hasn't been growing since the mid-1980s. Still, it is a clear plus for the province. Some of the minuses have been less well laid out. The infrastructure deficit is perhaps the largest; it was ignored for several years to make spending cuts look affordable. More and more, government and outside observers acknowledged the existence of this deficit starting in about 2000. One reason they began paying attention was the insistent call for help from Canadian cities, including cities in apparently rich Alberta.

The Klein-era Conservatives said they would get rid of the province's debt, without raising taxes. Most Alberta voters believed they did. However, the success story depended largely on who controlled the books. By 2004, cities were saying that years of cutting corners and putting off maintenance had built up a huge debt that was being tolerated merely because it was not on the province's financial accounts. The provincial government was driving to pay off all its debt in time for the province's centennial on September 1, 2005. Alberta's towns and cities were going to celebrate on pothole-ridden streets, cracked sidewalks, and in faded ice rinks.

Bruce Duncan, Edmonton's intergovernmental affairs officer, put the situation succinctly to his city council: "As the fiscal problem got better, our infrastructure situation got worse."

Alberta cities said they needed about $800 million a year for ten years to cover the gap between the existing level of maintenance and the level that was actually needed to keep roads, buildings, and utilities in decent repair.

Edmonton did a thorough review of those needs with the help of a framework developed by the Federation of Canadian Municipalities. The city found that by 2002 it had infrastructure needs worth $18 billion in replacement costs. Most of that was in the form of roads, sidewalks, and sewers—$8.1 billion in drainage works, and $5.2 billion in roads and sidewalks. The inventory found 58 per cent of total infrastructure assets could be classed as being in good condition, 29 per cent in fair condition, and 13 per cent in poor condition. Funding was so low that the city expected it would take fourteen years to repair or replace just the portion of assets rated in "poor" or "critical" condition.

These weren't straight-line matters either. A dollar of maintenance put off today could translate into a ten dollar cost tomorrow. The situation was most acute in roads. Patching up a lane of deteriorating ten-year-old road would cost about $8,000 per kilometre. Rebuilding an unmaintained thirteen-year-old road would cost about $200,000 per kilometre.

In total, the city of Edmonton expected in 2002 that it would have enough money to pay for about $165 million a year in infrastructure replacement over the next ten years. But, keeping the assets in reasonable shape would likely cost about $361 million. Edmonton would need an estimated $5.9 billion in infrastructure money between 2002 and 2012. Its available funding added up to $2.7 billion.

The $3.2 billion in unfunded infrastructure needs was a form of debt. It was a debt conveniently off the province's list of responsibilities and off the province's books.

Calgary was dealing with the same infrastructure debt—a painfully visible debt for the city, and a hidden one for the province. Calgary's 2004 budget allocated $1.4 billion to tax-supported capital projects for the coming five years. But, it identified another $1.38 billion in unfunded capital needs. Calgary planned to cope with at least some of these requirements by authorizing the borrowing of $350 million. Financial debt was going to be added to the debt consisting of construction and maintenance left undone. These debts were growing despite a concerted restraint effort that had led to a decline in Calgary's per-capita spending (in inflation-adjusted dollars) after 1985. Edmonton was also turning to real debt; in 2004, its city council authorized a program to borrow $50 million a year, and to raise taxes to provide the money to make payments on that debt.

The pressure on the cities was skewing the financial books to make members of the provincial government look like heroes. Much of the urban infrastructure deficit stemmed from growth. After the tough times of the early 1990s cleared away, people started migrating into Alberta from other provinces by the thousands again. Calgary grew by about 17,000 people a year from 1998 to 2002. Total housing starts in that period averaged 10,375 units a year, and 7,130 of those were single-family homes or duplexes, requiring relatively more services than apartments and condominiums. Edmonton was growing nearly as fast; in 2002 nearly 9,000 new homes were built in the city.

The sprawl of people and houses chewed up farmland and natural areas. Residential Calgary spread by just over 1,000 acres a year after growth took off in the mid-1990s. The availability of surrounding land was one of the factors that made housing in Alberta relatively cheaper than in British Columbia or Ontario, if you didn't count environmental losses, or the need to provide services to endless new subdivisions rather than to already serviced downtown areas.

This growth was putting more financial pressure on the cities than the need to maintain and replace old structures. By 2003, Edmonton estimated that 58 per cent of the unfunded projects it would ideally like to take on in the coming ten years were related to population growth, compared with 40 per cent related to rehabilitation of existing assets. Calgary estimated that 61 per cent of its unfunded infrastructure demands over the coming five years resulted from growth.

As officials in both cities were acutely aware, the addition of thousands of new people each year strained municipal budgets but was a financial bonus for the province. The difference lay in tax sources. The cities' biggest revenue source was property taxation, which did not keep up with the demands of growth. The province reaped hundreds of millions of dollars in extra income tax from the newcomers.

As the city of Calgary summed up in one of its budget documents in 2003: "Property taxes in particular do not keep pace with population and economic growth. And like all cities in Alberta, Calgary's property tax revenue is shared with the province for education costs. Like all cities, Calgary has very few revenue sources from which to draw to pay for the infrastructure that supports growth, while provincial and federal governments are almost 'growth proof': their revenue comes primarily from income taxes (personal and corporate), both of which increase during times of economic growth. The differences are dramatic. For example, in the decade between 1990 and 2000, on a per-capita basis and adjusted for inflation, Ottawa's income-tax revenue rose by 17 per cent and Alberta's by 32 per cent, while Calgary's tax revenue actually shrank by four per cent."

These numbers were a bargaining position and included a lot of assumptions. Aside from the difficulty of estimating future construction costs, there was the uncertainty of future needs. The cities' growth could slow down, eliminating some of the anticipated infrastructure deficit. Nor was the situation of Alberta cities unique. Most cities across the country could come up with lists of major infrastructure needs. The difference in Alberta was that oil and gas money was pouring into the province. A little was trickling back to the municipalities. The province decided to give Edmonton and Calgary a five-cent share of its nine-cents-a-litre gasoline tax for any gas sold within their boundaries. The sharing was authorized in 1999, was temporarily cut, and was finally restored in 2002. It was putting about $90 million a year into Calgary and slightly less into Edmonton.

The new transfers were not nearly big enough to change the general picture or to acknowledge the fact the cities were living with massive hidden debt. Billions of dollars were being put into the political goal of paying off the debt in time for the 100th birthday party. Accepting the existence of a multibillion-dollar "infrastructure deficit" would cheapen that achievement.

But this is Alberta. People are able to handle the existence of contradictory data—as long as no one asks them to repeat it out loud. Yes, the cities are living with a multibillion-dollar infrastructure deficit. Yes, universities have been talking about the same kind of deficit since the 1980s. And as a matter of fact, some arms of the provincial government were indicating by 2004 that they were also facing a growing infrastructure deficit.

The wake-up call seems to have arrived about the year 2000. That was when the federal government launched an infrastructure program for Alberta, with costs shared by Ottawa and the province. The 1999–2000 period also saw the provincial auditor general start demanding that government departments get a much better handle on the cost of deferred maintenance of physical assets. The government started adding up the bill, which turned out to be dismayingly huge. Even big bumps in spending were not enough to catch up.

The 2004 budget brought a sharp jump in capital spending, but the business plans for individual departments showed only a marginal improvement in many capital assets, and a further deterioration in highways.

The Learning Department expected that 55 per cent of elementary and high schools would be in "good" physical condition by 2007, compared with 52 per cent in 2003. Post-secondary institutions were going to erode—with an anticipated 45 per cent in "good" condition by 2007, down from 47 per cent in 2003. Health facilities, including seniors' lodges, stood to see a somewhat bigger improvement, rising to 64 per cent in "good" condition from 57 per cent.

But, the Transportation Department's 2004 business plan expected Alberta highways to deteriorate steadily over the next three years. The percentage of provincial highways in "good condition" was measured at 65 per cent in the fiscal year 2002–03. The target for 2004 was 62 per cent in good condition, sliding to 59.5 per cent in 2006–07. The percentage of highways in "poor condition" was targeted to rise to 16.5 per cent from 11.2 per cent over that same four-year period. By March 2004, "deferred preservation" work on provincial highways was estimated at $900 million. Those numbers should have resonated. One of the ways Albertans have thought of their province as being relatively prosperous over the last half-century has been to say the province's highways are better than the highways in Saskatchewan.

When a Liberal member of the legislature estimated the provincial government's overall infrastructure debt at $6 billion to $9 billion during the 2004 budget debate, Infrastructure Minister Ty Lund didn't dispute him. "Yes, we acknowledge that, and we have talked about it," Lund said. It doesn't make any sense to let buildings, roads, and other assets fall into disrepair, he added, although that had been an unspoken part of the government's financial strategy for a decade.

Alberta apparently had an overall provincial and municipal infrastructure debt somewhere about the size of its fabled Heritage Savings Trust Fund. How could those numbers fit with a belief that the province has paid off its debt? In one way, it was easy. One of the most firmly established principles of communication theory is that people all over the world resist facts that conflict with their beliefs. What makes up local character is the choice of which beliefs people cling to.

THE POVERTY OF LOCAL AUTHORITY

Any argument for transferring power from Ottawa to Alberta is an argument for local control of things that matter to people, and that are most efficiently or fairly administered at a local level.

This is not a question of regionalism. This is an organizing principle that every business and government must deal with. Health care is a prime example of a service the provinces can operate much better than a massive federal health department would. All kinds of other services are better handled at a more local level.

But, here's the Alberta paradox. Provincial politicians here are perfectly happy to demand a transfer of federal power to themselves. They are never happy to transfer power to a sub-provincial level. It goes against political instinct. In Alberta, letting local authorities have both money and power does more than violate political instinct. It cracks one of the three pillars of the Klein Revolution—privatization, flat taxes, and centralized control. The government has had ups and downs with privatization and flat taxes. There has been no such vacillation about centralized control.

Urban Cowboys

Towns and cities are the reality of modern Alberta. About two-thirds of the province's population lives in Calgary and the metropolitan Edmonton region. The 2001 federal census found 80 per cent of people in Alberta living in towns or cities big enough to qualify for Census Canada's definition of "urban." Alberta is the third most heavily urbanized province in Canada, just behind British Columbia (82-per-cent-urban according to the 2001 census, and Ontario (83-per-cent-urban in the 2001 census).

It continues to become even more urban. The cities have been growing faster than rural areas for decades. Successful rural centres have been transforming into urban places. Even the spaces between the cities have been filling in. The 300 kilometres between Edmonton and Calgary has become known as the Highway 2 Corridor.

The name recognizes the importance of this strip of land as the population and economic growth centre of the province. But, it also indicates a change in the character of this part of Alberta. Edmonton and Calgary used to be urban islands surrounded by a rural sea dotted here and there by smaller urban islands like Red Deer, Lethbridge, and Medicine Hat. Now the space along Highway 2, between the two large cities, has evolved into an urban archipelago. The built-up areas increasingly blend into one another. The major cities extend their economic and psychological reach. Even the road signs tell the story. These days, you can be out driving through uninhabited grazing land and come to a gravel road with a city-style street sign and number on it, rather than a highway sign.

When was the last time you saw Alberta described as an urban province? It doesn't sound right. The standard picture of an alienated West, or an irritable Alberta full of ranchers and energy executives, doesn't accommodate that reality. The standard picture doesn't even allow for Alberta municipal politicians speaking on a national stage, as many of them have started to do. Myth no longer squares with what you see when you walk down the province's main streets. When that happens, the real western alienation that you find in Alberta is a province alienated from itself.

Small Spenders

After the great upheaval of 1992–93, the Alberta government started saving money in a lot of ways. One of the most important was by squeezing the cities. The province drastically cut financial transfers to municipalities. And, it started taking money out of cities by taking over a share of municipal property taxes to help pay for education.

Through the late 1980s, local governments in Alberta relied on transfers from the province for little more than 20 per cent of their overall revenue. Local property taxes provided about 37 per cent of overall municipal revenues across the province.

That changed sharply starting in 1993. Municipal grants were among the prominent targets for spending cuts. Provincial transfers suddenly made up less than 15 per cent of overall municipal revenues in Alberta. Property taxes and related items filled the gap and suddenly accounted for about 42 per cent of all the towns' and cities' revenues. The province began filling in again as a construction boom emerged in the oil sands and bigger royalties on natural gas poured in. But, it did not restore much of the loss. By 2001, provincial transfers reached 15.9 per cent of overall revenues for all Alberta municipalities. They had been 21.9 per cent in 1988.

How did municipalities cope? They cut spending. They also benefited from debt control and from the general drop in interest rates that made all government debt easier to bear through the 1990s. Debt charges as a percentage of total municipal spending in Alberta fell to 7.1 per cent in 2001 from 17.4 per cent in 1988. Many municipalities raised property taxes and service fees, as well.

The changes in taxation and spending were significant. Property taxes took up 2.9 per cent of personal disposable income in the province in 2001, compared with 1.8 per cent in 1988—an increase of more than 50 per cent. Spending control was equally apparent. Municipal program spending in 2001 amounted to 15.8 per cent of overall provincial and local program spending in Alberta, compared with 17.8 per cent in 1988. The municipalities' success in controlling costs was, if anything, more spectacular than that of the province, which enjoyed billions in new energy revenues.

The sharp drop in urban debt in the 1990s and early 2000s could have led to lower municipal property taxes. Instead, towns and cities watched helplessly as the province in effect scooped up all the savings by reducing its grants to them. The municipalities were left no better off than before. Their taxes had to be stabilized or increased because of missing provincial transfers.

Most of the numbers above were summarized in a report to Edmonton city council in April 2004 by Mel McMillan and Paul Boothe, economists at the University of Alberta. McMillan told the councillors what had happened to the money saved by the city's years of paying off debt: "The province basically captured that fiscal dividend by cutting transfers."

When the federal government captured money, Alberta and the other provinces yelled for their share. When the Alberta government captured money from its cities, not much happened. There wasn't even agreement on whether making a noise in public was a good idea.

In one way, the financial squeeze was unremarkable. Boothe and McMillan pointed out that every province except Quebec had cut transfers to municipalities starting in the early 1990s. It was part of a cross-Canada effort to get public finances under control.

The ordinariness of Alberta's situation might have surprised the average Alberta voter. People here are always caught in a dilemma of wanting to be unique. That's part of the Alberta mystique: real Albertans always go their own way. It's been part of the provincial government's mystique, too. They sold the impression that they were uniquely vigorous and successful in controlling taxes and spending. So it's difficult for them to justify their actions on municipal finance by saying, "Well, everyone else did it. We all had no choice."

Power Shift

The roots of the Klein-era consolidation of power over local authorities go deep into the constant transformation of Prairie society. The rapid development of the rural areas of the Prairie provinces peaked by the late 1920s. After that came decades of ever-increasing concentration of wealth and population. Farms kept growing bigger. People gathered into larger towns. The physical assets needed to support their society dwindled, but the governing structures did not shrink as fast. School boards ran fewer schools. Hospital boards ran small buildings, each with its own administrative staff. In the general panic over Alberta's finances in 1992–93, a lot of people looked at these arrangements and decided they no longer made sense. There was a lot of public support for trimming the number of school boards and for consolidating about 200 hospital boards into sixteen regional health authorities. What was not anticipated was the other side of rationalization—concentration of power in the hands of provincial politicians.

In the early days of the Klein Revolution, the government begin systematically expanding its control of what had been or could have been local decision making.

The province interfered freely in local affairs. During the 1990s, it amalgamated, then split municipal governments in the Lac La Biche-Bonnyville area. It conducted reviews of municipal governments in the towns of Calmar and Olds. Local governments found huge portions of their budgets subject to the whims of provincial cabinet ministers. Policing costs became a major sore point, and towns and cities were increasingly left on their own. In one extreme case, the central Alberta town of Lac La Biche, just slightly too big to qualify for provincial money, was spending more than half its budget on police costs by 2003. It coped by letting roads and sidewalks crumble. Help finally arrived the following year. The province created new police grants. Characteristically, the money came with a twist. Out of the total $41.5 million in new transfers from the province, $12 million would go to a new and vaguely described provincial co-ordination of police services. Money was flowing to towns and cities, but the provincial government would take more control.

In time, the federal government stepped in to help on the money side. The province reacted ambivalently, welcoming the money but jealously guarding its authority. The federal 2004 budget announcement that municipalities would be exempted from paying the goods and services tax was acceptable. Prime Minister Paul Martin's announcement a few weeks later that Ottawa intended to rebate five cents a litre from its gasoline tax to municipalities caused more of a stir. Premier Ralph Klein's first response was a grumpy suspicion that the provinces would be expected to kick in their own rebates. When that did not turn out to be true, the province fell back on saying the federal government could give municipalities a gas tax rebate, but would first have to negotiate an agreement with the province setting down the terms.

Higher Learning

Universities were subject to the same impulse of control. As with the cities, Alberta's post-secondary institutions had plenty of company in other provinces coping with the hard-bitten 1990s. But, the tightening of their budgets reflected some Alberta peculiarities.

First was the ambivalent attitude that many members of the government had toward post-secondary education. Alberta was a province led by a high-school dropout, albeit one with much more natural ability than his skimpy formal education indicated. A number of government ministers and MLAs had either not gone to university or had not finished. Even among the graduates, there was sometimes a tendency to scoff at academics or to view universities as a suspect urban graft onto the sturdy down-home character of what they saw as the essential Albertan.

At the same time, all the rhetoric about economic development pointed to a need for the skills that post-secondary education supplied. Cabinet ministers knew that. The trick was how to get the benefits of universities while holding down costs and keeping the pesky professors under control. The answer was similar to the formula applied in municipal government: make the users pay more and impose new control over the institutions.

Funding had already been squeezed in the 1980s. The premier post-secondary institution in the province is the University of Alberta. Its business plan for 2004 showed a long decline in provincial government grants starting in 1981. Grants per full-time-equivalent student were pushing $15,000 a year (measured in inflation-adjusted 2002 dollars) in the 1980–81 fiscal year. They slid to about $12,000 by mid-decade, with a noticeable drop in 1987–88, the year after oil prices collapsed. The next significant drop began with the post-1992 spending cuts and was never reversed. In 2002–2003, provincial grants per full-time equivalent student were about $8,000 a year. In constant 2002 dollars, Alberta was contributing less money to the university's operating revenues in 2002–03 ($293.3 million) than in 1980–81 ($309.4 million.) The university's operating revenues per full-time student dropped to $13,348 in 2002–03 from $16,867 in 1980–81.

One way the university coped was by squeezing more students into each class. The 1980s began with 13.7 full-time students for each faculty member. Twenty-two years later, the student-faculty ratio was 22.8 to one.

A big shift also took place in tuition and fee payments. Fees had been creeping up in the 1980s. After 1992, they took off. Tuition and other fees generated $31.6 million for the University of Alberta in 1980–81 and $134.1 million in 2002–03. The average student's tuition fees and related costs tripled in a decade.

The province was holding down its spending by the same method that it was using on municipalities—transferring costs rather than cutting them.

Needs still went unmet. The University of Alberta forecast an operating deficit of $3.8 million in its 2004 budget. That was the third straight budget for which the university had received provincial permission to run a deficit. And one-time revenue was papering over a much bigger underlying deficit—university officials were calling it a "revenue gap"—estimated at more like $28.7 million.

The chronic shortfalls in maintenance of post-secondary buildings and equipment were just slightly more in the public eye. The indifferent maintenance of existing physical plants was partly offset by construction of new buildings. But, this came with different costs. It was an open secret among university staff and students that administrators were competing for government money for new construction while letting the teaching effort slide; the University of Alberta's engineering faculty was a prime example. The university was also coping with a new unpredictability in funding that hurt efforts to attract the top scientific researchers who were needed to expand the province's economy.

The government found itself in a dilemma that kept cropping up because of Alberta's peculiarities.

On the one hand, it wanted to run important public services more like a business. It wanted those service areas separated from politics, usually by keeping them in the control of arm's-length agencies or boards. But, separation ran counter to the government's grasping tendencies. Provincial politicians also wanted more and more control of the institutions they were superficially trying to make more independent.

One fallback was to insert senior political figures into the boards of governors of post-secondary institutions. These had typically been places where Progressive Conservative supporters could expect appointment. By the early 2000s, the appointments increasingly went to people who were more than supporters; they pulled the levers in some of its most important political control rooms.

Reading the board membership lists almost always yielded a name or two that sounded like a commissar. You could find on the University of Alberta board of governors: Jim Edwards, a former member of Parliament; Brian Heidecker, a rancher with a long history of involvement with both the federal and provincial Conservative parties; Ove Minsos, a sometime local riding executive; Wendy Kinsella, one of the few unsuccessful Conservative candidates in the 2001 provincial election. (Kinsella also became chair of the board of NorQuest College, a high-school upgrading and skills training institution.) At the University of Calgary were former MPs Bobbie Sparrow and Rod Love, who had been Klein's former chief of staff for many years. The University of Lethbridge board featured Gord Rosko, a former communications director in the Treasury Department and a key member of the party's Calgary "war room" during the 2001 election. Mount Royal College in Calgary had Jack Ady, who had served as Klein's minister of advanced education in the early '90s, and Jack Davis, chief executive officer of the Calgary health region and Klein's former deputy minister of cabinet (head of the province's civil service). At the Southern Alberta Institute of Technology in Calgary, there was Ivan Bernardo, who had worked five years in Klein's office as head of caucus liaison and cabinet policy co-ordinator. The Northern Alberta Institute of Technology had former Klein cabinet minister Jon Havelock. Grant MacEwan Community College in Edmonton saw former candidate and provincial party president Eric Young become chairman of a board that included Hal Danchilla, a former assistant to cabinet ministers, including Stockwell Day; Danchilla had also been a national campaign manager for Day in the Alliance party and later a campaign manager for Tony Clement's bid for the leadership of the new Conservative Party of Canada. Grande Prairie Regional College had Vi Sunohara, a former party constituency executive. Olds College featured former

Conservative party president Alf Savage as board chairman for a while; former MLA Gary Severtson later became a board member.

By 2003, the urge to control the post-secondaries developed into a more overt and sweeping plan. A new law was proposed that would merge the functions of Alberta universities and colleges. While still nominally self-governing, they would operate under the umbrella of what looked like a rudimentary school board for post-secondary institutions, to be known as Campus Alberta. The minister in charge of the recently renamed Learning Department would have powers similar to a board superintendent and chairman.

The bill passed. It gave the minister the power to approve the "mandate" of each institution and to make it stick solely to that mandate. A Campus Alberta Accreditation and Co-ordination Board would advise the minister on any proposals for study programs. The minister would in effect determine which courses and programs each university and college should offer, although little in the way of new money would follow. To accomplish this task, the bill also gave the minister the power to determine which skills would be needed in Alberta in the future.

A commentary from the private consulting firm Cambridge Strategies Inc. concluded: "Bill 43 enables and empowers the minister of learning to ensure the government returns to playing a substantial role in picking winners and losers in the Alberta economy of the future. . . . Bill 43 effectively revives the forsaken government role of centralized planning, controlling and directing the economy."

Health Care

Sometimes it's tough to tell in Alberta whether the tail wags the dog in health care, or the dog wags the tail. But, the province tries hard to keep control.

The government created sixteen regional health authorities as part of its post-1992 reforms. Over the next several years, it also wiped out much of the policy function in the Health Department and subjected the department to several reorganizations that took place about once a year. On top of that, the premier's office cleared out the entire senior management of the department in 2000 in retribution for the embarrassing loss of a public debate over Bill 11, an attempt to establish regulations for private surgery clinics.

The health authorities held some real power. A number of the rural health regions successfully resisted having to make as deep budget cuts as Calgary or Edmonton in the mid-1990s. They were allowed to adapt gradually. And, the province as a whole was rich enough to avoid the overt closure of rural hospitals that made budget balancing a much tougher task politically in Saskatchewan. Rural hospitals tended to switch from acute care to longer-term care, but they stayed open. The government's pretensions to ruthless business-like management gave way before the realities of health politics.

This was one of the grandest of the self-deceptions during the Klein era. The party line had Alberta leading the country in "bold" changes to health care. The reality was an enduring Alberta pattern that had seen the old Social Credit dynasty cement its support in the newly prosperous 1950s by putting money into health, education, and highways. The conflict between the appearance and the reality led by the spring of 2004 to an admission from Premier Ralph Klein that real health reform had not occurred despite several government assertions that it had.

In some ways, however, the regional health authorities were creating new solutions. A troubled early consolidation of hospital services in Edmonton was brought under control with the arrival in the mid-1990s of a new regional chief executive, Sheila Weatherill. Big organizational schemes gave way to practical action on smaller-scale concrete issues. The Edmonton region turned heads in the national health community by creating a phone-in health advice line staffed twenty-four hours a day by nurses; the phone line provided an important health service while reducing the strain on emergency departments. The region also created transitional seniors' care and picked up on years of work by local community leaders by creating innovative primary-care health centres—an alternative to expensive new hospital space.

There were limits, however. The Calgary and Edmonton regions each ran about one-third of the overall health system. They were big enough that they could have become essentially autonomous, replacing the provincial Health Department within their own borders. That was never going to happen.

The assertion of control over health regions began with questions about the way some were being run. The usual problems involved internal staff conflicts and budget overruns. The first sign was the replacement of almost the entire Edmonton health authority in 1996, two years after the first board was appointed. There was never a public explanation but the board was, in effect, fired. Health ministers also conducted reviews of the authorities that looked after the Leduc–Drayton Valley and Grande Prairie–Peace River regions, and fired the Lakeland regional board in the area northeast of Edmonton.

The health regions often pleaded financial poverty, too. The province cut deeply into health in the first great sweep of post-1992 restructuring. Spending on health was slashed to $3.77 billion in fiscal 1995–96 from $4.3 billion in 1992–93. The cuts were reversed in time for the 1997 election, and health spending started climbing again every year.

Yet, there never seemed to be enough. Some of the regions with the best political connections were the most likely to plead for more. Calgary ran chronic deficits and demanded a bigger share of the health budget. In this environment, the government habitually played a two-sided game. Political leaders told voters they were getting good health care, which was in many ways true. On the other hand, they took every chance available to say that health finances were out of control. A favourite tactic—transparently misleading but used often—was to measure the growth of the health budget against the record low levels reached in 1995–96. That exaggerated the long-term rate of growth wildly. Cabinet ministers and MLAs never let this criticism bother them. Nor were they bothered that long-term budget numbers did not seem to support another of their favourite claims—that the province's health spending was rising at a faster rate than its revenues.

Their response to another measure of health spending was more curious. Going back more than twenty years, the province's health budget used up a more or less constant share of the economy—just over four per cent of Alberta's gross domestic product. A legislature committee studying the 2004 provincial budget asked Health Minister Gary Mar about that flat long-term trend. He said the ratio was "a bit of a red herring. I don't think that the expression of health care expenditures as a percentage of gross domestic product is a particularly useful measure of anything." In fact, it is commonly used by health economists around the world. (There was stark contradiction here, too. Mar's logic took the province's position on the control of greenhouse gases under the Kyoto accord and turned it upside down. Alberta had explicitly called for a link between the amount of allowed greenhouse gas emissions and size of the economy as measured by gross domestic product.)

Alberta suffered from the same health-care conundrum as the rest of the country: how can anyone control spending on a service in which spending could be limitless? The difference in Alberta was a perpetual tendency to want to go in two directions at once. The government bemoaned the cost of paying doctors and nurses, but offered the kind of pay that would lure both from other provinces. It demanded more federal money for health care, but fought any federal role in monitoring or decision making. It talked constantly about reforming the health system, but constantly met political needs by injecting more money into the system.

The last point was the most painful. The Alberta government played a large role in prompting passage of the Canada Health Act by tolerating physicians' extra-billing in the early 1980s. It reluctantly acquiesced to the federal ban on extra-billing. But, during the next two decades, any discussion of health reform in the province almost invariably included some proposals to have people pay more.

Basic Education

For schools around the province the story was the same—uncertain funding and a perpetual tendency to concentrate more power in the hands of the provincial government. The first signs of more aggressive authority emerged shortly after the 1993 election. Part of the change for school boards was new ministerial power over the appointment of district superintendents of education. Ten years later, the government was still hanging on to that power, refusing to give it back.

The province had also dealt with a nagging problem of differences in local capacities to pay for education by taking control of education property taxes from individual school boards and dividing the money according to needs. That solved the equity problem but left local boards without much in the way of effective power. It also created a huge political problem for municipal councillors.

Every year, the government sends Alberta municipalities a notice saying how much property tax they have to raise for education in their area. The education levy generally amounts to about 40 per cent of local property tax. That soaks up a lot of the towns' and cities' only significant tax source. And, it sticks municipal councillors with the political responsibility for collecting more than $1 billion, which ends up in the hands of the province.

The provincial education tax also turned into a broken promise. The government originally pledged to keep adjusting mill rates so that the overall revenue from the education portion of property tax did not increase. In 2002, it decided to let that revenue start creeping up. At the same time, the province stuck to a pledge not to let its income from beer and liquor sales climb beyond the levels reached when the privatization of alcohol retailing was announced in 1993.

The school boards have to live on a budget controlled by the province. The boards also have to live with cabinet ministers throwing their weight around—just as they do with health authorities. The education minister fired the entire Calgary public school board in the summer of 1999 after repeated internal disagreements among its members. The board had arguably become dysfunctional (a curious fate in the city that was supposed to be the epitome of business efficiency in Alberta). Squabbles, demands for reprimands, a physical confrontation, and catty notes passed around at board meetings demeaned its public image. The government also thought the board was wasting $35 million a year because it signed a contract giving teachers a say in the size of student-teacher ratios in the classroom. A provincial cabinet minister firing a major local authority was still a drastic step. To bridge the gap until the next board election, he appointed as trustee George Cornish, who had been a senior city official when Klein was Calgary's mayor.

A bitter strike by about 22,000 public school teachers in 2002 left school boards wedged between teachers demanding higher pay without compromises on class size, and a provincial government determined to hold down salary costs. Teachers eventually settled for an agreement that included arbitration. That third-party study gave them a salary increase well beyond what the government expected. The province refused to boost its education budget enough in 2003 to pay the extra cost and school boards cut hundreds of teachers from their payrolls to make do. When the Edmonton public board said it would have to lay off teachers, the education minister peremptorily ordered an audit of its books (which found none of the financial waste he implied was there). In the summer of 2004, the government announced a crash plan to hire more than 1,300 teachers around the province. An election was around the corner.

As in health care, Alberta cabinet ministers were putting a new meaning into the phrase "The buck stops here." For them, it meant decentralization stopped at the door to their offices. Power had to be decentralized in Canada. In Alberta, it had to be concentrated in the provincial cabinet.

Building a New Alberta

Despite the chronic disputes over money and the accumulation of power in the hands of the provincial government, many local authorities in Alberta were performing well.

The University of Alberta consistently showed up near the top of ratings of Canadian post-secondary schools with the University of Calgary not far behind.

Alberta students consistently did well in international and Canada-wide comparisons of achievement test results. Edmonton won awards for the management tools it was developing to keep track of its infrastructure needs and determine which were most important. Alberta physicians were helping develop alternatives to the standard fee-for-service payment system. The Edmonton health region was winning recognition across the country as a leader not only in containing costs but for its innovations.

The notable common thread in all these achievements was their dependence on high-quality local leadership. That may have had to do with a habit of dealing with mundane realities rather than with hot air. While provincial leaders fought with federal politicians or passed laws naming the bull trout as Alberta's official fish, and ammolite as Alberta's official gem, and a certain pattern of plaid as Alberta's official tartan, local leaders had to figure out where people making ten dollars an hour were going to live. They had to figure out how to thin out crowds in hospital emergency rooms.

Local authorities had to confront change head-on. A town like Brooks, once a quiet place centred on farm and oilfield activity, had to turn itself into a home for hundreds of workers, mostly immigrants, earning ten to seventeen dollars an hour in a huge local meat processing plant. The town had to provide cheap housing, and it did.

Other towns went through slow, bureaucratic grinds in an effort to cope with the changing world around them. One of them was Lacombe, a town of nearly 10,000 located just north of Red Deer, about at the midpoint of the Highway 2 Corridor.

Lacombe was a thriving place built around grain and livestock farms, a local college, and an agricultural research station. Its pretty downtown and distinctive, historic buildings drew professionals looking for a pleasant place to live.

Not everyone in this new Alberta was sharing the general prosperity, however. By the early 2000s, local volunteers were beginning to organize an effort to create housing for people who couldn't make ends meet in a province at the top of Canada's economic ladder.

Some of those in trouble had mental health or other health difficulties and were living on $855 a month from the province's Assured Income for the Severely Handicapped program. Some were single parents. Some worked in ten-dollar-an-hour jobs. A number had been getting help from families no longer able or willing to help. All were faced with a paradox. There was plenty of vacant housing in Lacombe, but much of it was space in battered apartments, and most of it was high-cost. Prices were influenced by levels set in Edmonton and Calgary, and by the ability of more affluent residents to pay.

A TD Bank study of the Edmonton-Calgary corridor in 2003 said a divergence between rich and poor Albertans was a problem that could affect future economic growth. The housing market in places like Lacombe was one local expression of that general concern.

The people affected did not like to advertise their situation. They showed up first at places like the Lacombe food bank, which had a client list of 500. While the province was booming, the local food bank's client list grew by 43 per cent through 2001 and another 20 per cent through 2002.

People in financial trouble also showed up at the town's community resource centre, called Neighbourhood Place and run by Michelle Baer. "People come to see us in our office when they run out of resources," she said in an interview. "They are scrambling. They're paying their utilities one month, their rent next, they're going to the food bank. . . . It's when people realize there's no grocery money, that's when they come for help."

Baer and several other volunteers from local social service agencies, church groups, the local health unit, the town, and real estate firms became members of the Lacombe Housing Initiative. It won a $16,000 grant from the Alberta Real Estate Foundation to pay for a housing needs study. That assessment opened the eyes of many people in Lacombe. It estimated that as many as 880 households in the town might be suffering hardship because of housing costs. An estimated 550 households were paying 30 per cent to 49 per cent of their gross (before-tax) income for shelter. As many as 330 more might be facing housing costs that ate up more than half their gross income.

And, the superficially prosperous town was developing an income split becoming characteristic of large parts of Alberta. The town's households tended to gather in two income groups: one between $15,000 and $30,000 a year and the other earning more than $60,000 a year. The province as a whole was tending to follow the same pattern although the larger cities had more people with incomes under $15,000 or over $100,000. Anyone with a ten-dollar-an-hour job was not going to survive without a good second income in the family.

The less affluent families got along from month to month with help from the network of community volunteers and social service agencies that is probably small-town Alberta's greatest secret. Most towns of any size in the province have a thriving society of service clubs, church groups, support groups, and other agencies of all kinds, as well as offices of the provincially funded Family and Community Support Services. When people came to Neighbourhood Place after running down to their last jar of peanut butter, Baer was able to draw on FCSS emergency food vouchers, help from churches, occasional corporate donations, and local thrift stores.

The Community Housing Initiative wanted to replace these emergency stopgaps with townhouses for thirty families. The idea was to get people into stable situations where they could also start working on their education and, ideally, put a little money into escrow accounts for down payments on homes or for a set of tools for a job. The Lacombe Foundation was putting together a $1.5-million funding proposal for what the local volunteers hoped would be a housing demonstration project for central Alberta. The money would come from the federal-provincial Affordable Housing Initiative, with each senior government sharing the cost equally.

But, the program rules said the town had to be involved. That put Mayor Bill McQuesten and his council into a tough spot. For a start, he wanted to avoid having the town take over the project: "This has to be a grassroots initiative. . . . There needs to be buy-in from the community in order to make it fit somewhere."

Beyond that, he did not want a big financial commitment to something under federal and provincial jurisdiction: "Financially, municipalities are stretched to the limits right now. . . . Municipalities don't have the responsibility to pay for any of it. But the issue is that this needs to be addressed."

So, the town was willing to put in token initial support while trying to avoid crossing the line into a permanent commitment of money. The town thought money should be flowing the other way.

McQuesten supported proposals by Alberta municipalities for a share of both gasoline taxes and resource revenues. He worried about a new pipeline the Lacombe region would soon need to carry water from the Red Deer River; the line would cost about $25 million and the province intended to pay only for half. He was not eager to take on housing when other issues were pressing.

But, he also saw community housing as a need "in a capitalist society that is founded on biblical principles." Lacombe had a strong social conscience, he said.

It was a place where, although the population had ballooned to 10,000, "you don't know everybody, but you certainly still wave to everybody. . . . There are people right out of school making minimum wage, and they need a place to live." At the same time, the council had to remember other people earning a few thousand dollars too much to qualify for help: "How do they feel when they're not getting the same breaks?" It was a tough nut for the town.

In 2004, the Community Housing Initiative was into its fifth year on the housing project. The effort was leading to a grant application that had to be sent to the Alberta Seniors Department. When asked who had to be convinced that the project was a good idea, Baer and another volunteer simultaneously said, "Stan Woloshyn."

Woloshyn was minister in charge of the Seniors Department. After the multiple layers of regulations were dealt with, and the many preliminary steps taken, years of effort came down to the wielding of raw political power by one man in a far richer government located about 125 kilometres up the highway. While he waited for the bureaucratic papers to land on his desk, a community tried to deal with the consequences of growing from a small town on the Prairies into a small city in an urban corridor—without access to more money or more power to deal with those consequences.

The provincial government was far more interested in accumulating both political commodities than in dishing them out.

THE POVERTY OF ALBERTA POLITICS

Alberta's massive wealth has paradoxically created a province of political poverty.

Alberta voters and politicians have created what is, for all practical purposes, a one-party state. This serves the purposes of many political campaigners and of many voters. A strong economy buys political disengagement. But when the government goes in directions voters disagree with, their only recourse is to express anger. If anger doesn't work, they are left with despair.

Alienation begins at home. It means alienation from politics inside Alberta as much as it means alienation from politics in Ottawa. The poverty of Alberta politics will continue as long as people in Alberta keep shutting their eyes to that truth.

Eating Humble Pie

The Alberta myth's centre of gravity settles somewhere around the image of the self-reliant cowboy or maverick entrepreneur—proud and independent people all. That myth is built on grains of truth and a tough history. The oil and gas industry was built by gutty entrepreneurs who wouldn't give up after Canadian banks refused their loan requests. Farmers living under constant risk of illness and bankruptcy built a viable agriculture industry in an often inhospitable land. But now the myth has also become the creation of journalists sticking to familiar story lines or trading co-operation for stories, and of politicians who have built their careers on submissive loyalty to their leader.

There isn't much room for pride in Alberta's public life. Often, there is barely room for self-respect. When you belong to a gang or live in a town run by a gang, you learn to accept the rituals of humility.

Every now and then this compulsive conformity gets put on public display. In the spring of 2004, Premier Ralph Klein got himself into a mess over whether one of the essays he had written for a distance-learning course he was taking at Athabasca University featured inadequate citation of sources. Some critics were throwing around accusations of plagiarism, although the evidence fell rather short on that score. Within days, the presidents of the University of Alberta and the University of Calgary had letters published in the *Edmonton Journal* and *Calgary Herald* applauding the premier for setting an example of the ideal of lifelong learning. The coincidence was noticed. Learning Minister Lyle Oberg quickly admitted that he had engaged four university presidents in a telephone call—Athabasca University and the University of Lethbridge were included—and suggested that they defend the academic integrity of the institutions. He pointedly called them "my institutions." The intervention did not help Klein and ended up hurting the university presidents' credibility. Some people were affronted, but the episode seemed routine. Public displays of submission were a fact of public life in Alberta, for big fish and for minnows.

Calgary Mayor David Bronconnier had gone a long way toward becoming a local politician nearly as popular in his city as Klein had been in his day as Calgary's mayor. Young and energetic, he strongly backed the position of the Alberta Urban Municipalities Association that cities should receive 20 per cent of any provincial government surplus. In April 2004, he criticized the province for not including such a provision in its new budget—despite a string of multibillion-dollar provincial surpluses—and did so with a much noticed comment comparing the budget to Ripley's Believe It or Not.

Klein sent him a stiff public message, underlined by one of his occasional lapses into coarse language: "It doesn't serve any useful purpose for any mayor of any municipality to go out of his or her way to get the government PO'd." Three days later, Bronconnier made headlines and television newscasts across the province with an apology during a speech to the Urban Development Institute. Bronconnier said he did not want to offend Klein or Klein's cabinet. "So today I withdraw my criticisms. I want to assure my provincial colleagues that it's not my intention to PO the provincial government." His remarks resonated in Edmonton, where Mayor Bill Smith was finishing a third term in office. Smith's tenure had featured an acknowledged preference for backroom diplomacy with provincial legislators rather than the conflict that had marred the shorter career of his predecessor, Jan Reimer.

Bronconnier's retreat was no radical departure. Criticizing the governing party in public had become unacceptable. Klein had felt no similar qualms during the early 1980s, when he was mayor and was badgering the provincial cabinet for hundreds of millions of dollars to expand Calgary's light rail transit system. Bronconnier also happened to have run as a Liberal in the 1997 federal election. That was like throwing pepper on the places he rubbed raw on the government's skin. But, even friends of the government experienced what it was like to break with the party line.

Eric Newell, for years the chairman of the Syncrude oil sands operation, received a frosty reception when he spoke at a provincial Conservative convention in the mid-1990s and urged party members to reconsider the importance of post-secondary education during a period of spending cuts. Bob Stollery, who led the development of PCL Construction from a local Edmonton firm to an international giant, took up the cause of child poverty after he retired. In September 2001, he spoke to an Edmonton audience made up of the local legal, business, and political establishment. Taking off from the government's catch-phrase "the Alberta Advantage," he asked where the Advantage was for the estimated 20 per cent of Albertans he said were getting poorer instead of richer. Three months later, he told an interviewer that while many had praised him for speaking out, a number of well-off people had called and accused him of not being a team player. "A team player," he said. "Can you imagine that, when we're talking about child poverty? I suppose anyone who criticizes the status quo is not a team player." In Alberta, that was true.

Public life was even tougher for those outside the governing circle. Brian Bechtel ran as a Liberal in the March 2001 provincial election and lost by 141 votes in a downtown Edmonton constituency. That fall, he won a seat on the Edmonton regional health authority, known as the Capital Health Authority. Being chosen by the public did not guarantee him the right to become the public's voice, he reported in the magazine *Alberta Views* in May 2003, two months after health authority elections were abolished. He said CHA board chairman Neil Wilkinson quickly told the new, elected members that debates were to be kept behind closed doors, public meetings were to be carefully stage-managed, and board members were to support all board decisions; doing otherwise would undermine staff and public confidence.

What that meant was made clear during a "rude awakening" following the release of the Mazankowski report on health care. Bechtel gave his impressions of the report when asked for them by a reporter from the *Edmonton Journal.* "I then received a call from Neil Wilkinson. He said that I should not have given that interview and that I should have referred the call to the PR people at the CHA. At a meeting shortly afterwards, many members of the board agreed with Neil's position. People like former city councillor and unsuccessful PC candidate Wendy Kinsella raised the possibility of my 'censure.'"

Bechtel's article sparked no public comment. Albertans knew the rules and usually lived by them. When a case of mad cow disease (BSE) was discovered in northern Alberta in 2003, Klein made a widely noted remark that a real Alberta rancher confronted with a sick cow might have followed the code of ranch country: "Shoot, shovel, and shut up." It was the code of Alberta politics, too.

That was never more true than during the height of hysteria over the Kyoto accord, in September 2002. Dr. David Swann, the medical officer of health for the Palliser Health Authority, in the Medicine Hat region of southeastern Alberta, publicly joined a campaign to urge federal ratification of the accord to control greenhouse gases. He said it was a health issue. A week later, the health region's board fired him. The Palliser board, like all the others in Alberta, reflected a heavy political influence. Len Mitzel, its chairman, was also a county reeve and president of Environment Minister Lorne Taylor's Progressive Conservative constituency association.

Taylor initially denied involvement. A day later he conceded he had telephoned Mitzel, but merely to seek clarification of what appeared to be a board stand on Kyoto that had left him "really shocked." Swann's case departed from the usual course. The firing drew widespread criticism and national media attention. Environmentalists said such tactics would undermine the government's position on Kyoto. The president of the Alberta Public Health Association said the firing "sends a message which could have a chilling effect on our ability to recruit" medical officers of health. The president of the Alberta Medical Association said the firing was "pretty scary" and a threat to doctors speaking out on health issues. Four days after Swann's dismissal was announced, Klein said medical officers of health had a right to speak out on Kyoto and other public issues "without fear of reprisal." The point was it had taken unusually sustained, widespread pressure to prompt that statement. Swann was offered his job back but declined. In August 2004, he decided to run for a Liberal nomination, saying, "I realized how fragile our democracy is."

No one was immune, however. Former cabinet minister Ernie Isley was one of the first prominent Progressive Conservatives to back Ralph Klein's bid for the party leadership in 1992. In 2003, he was dumped from the chairmanship of the Lakeland Health Authority in east-central Alberta after repeatedly criticizing the government for not providing what he thought was enough money for his region. He lost the chairmanship at the same time that health board elections were abolished. (He did, however, remain on the board and on another government-appointed agency, the Northern Alberta Development Council.) Isley had thought elections and debate were part of the democratic process: "If there's a little controversy and conflict, that tells me democracy is working. . . . People are upset that this government is arrogant enough to dismiss elected people. The question is, who's next?"

But, going along with authority had become the Albertan way. People who took on the government in public lost public jobs, private business, and personal reputation. Alberta's "maverick" image was mostly show, or maybe a wistful reaching for self-respect.

Who Cares?

It wasn't a secret. The government never minded everyone knowing the rules. Rich Vivone, publisher of a newsletter on Alberta politics, wrote in *Alberta Views* in 2004 that municipalities, school boards, and other groups had "been slapped around for years" with no response other than an occasional whimper.

Why the puzzling silence? He had asked. "When the question was raised with school trustees, the answer was downcast eyes and a shrug. When the question was raised with municipal councillors, the answer was more expressive—fear that the provincial government will 'get even' with organizations that dare criticize it in public. How will they get even? Meetings with MLAs are tougher to get, letters get lost, requests aren't heard, grant money takes longer to arrive, and information channels break down. Conservative MLAs aren't shy about it; groups that complain in public won't get a sympathetic ear."

Federal politicians could be and sometimes were arrogant in their dealings with Alberta. But, they were never accused of the petty and highly personal kind of bullying that provincial politicians sometimes indulged in. Why could the government in Ottawa count on rejection while the government in Edmonton could count on submission—from the same voters?

The provincial government spent money skilfully. The approximately $4 billion in electricity and natural gas handouts just before the 2001 election was the most spectacular example, but far from the only one. The federal government only occasionally had that kind of direct impact on people's lives.

Leadership also counted. Premier Ralph Klein was a construction of many individuals' hopes and dreams. They had made a psychological commitment to the image of Klein as a man of the people. Once they made that choice, it was difficult to pull back: they would have to admit they were wrong; there was no unanimously popular alternative in sight anyway. One letter to a newspaper articulated the commitment well: "The academics and the high foreheads in the media just can't stand to see an ordinary guy in a position of power. How is it possible for someone with so little education to be where Ralph Klein is, leader of the most successful government in Canada? Get used to it. Most of the rich people in the world are just like Ralph; they know how to relate to the ordinary guy and possess outstanding people skills, something academics see no need for, and are thus forced to exist in their own little world."

There was curious reasoning here, aside from the fact that it would have made Prime Minister Paul Martin, one of the "rich," as much a man of the people as Ralph Klein. Klein had entered public life not as an ordinary person but by building on his position as a popular Calgary media figure. By the time the letter to the editor was written, he was spending much of his spare time golfing and fishing with corporate executives. Some of the hobnobbing took place on trips to the high-priced British Columbia fishing lodge in which he had been allowed to buy an ownership stake on undisclosed terms. He had fashioned a self-image as a master politician and often gave reporters short lectures on political tactics.

He also carefully limited his displays of disdain to acceptable objects of ridicule—generally either protesters or members of opposition parties. So, he indulged regularly in comments like these to a Liberal member of the legislature asking in question period about auto insurance: "You know, the reason there are seventy-three of us and only five of them is that we listen to people. . . . He doesn't get it. That's why there are only five of them, and after the next election there will be even fewer." A few minutes later, he asked of the opposition MLA: "Is he deaf or just stupid?"

Klein apologized for the last remark after the Speaker of the legislature said it could suggest the MLA was handicapped. It had been only a somewhat sharper variation of the answers common in question period. It was typical of Klein's reaction when pressed on a sore point. Irked a number of times by the Parkland Institute, a think tank located at the University of Alberta, Klein wrote to university president Rod Fraser in 1999 to complain about what he termed the institute's "one-sided and ideologically biased attacks" and about its "anti-Alberta studies." Those comments in turn reflected a wider habit evident in Alberta's public discourse, one tinged with an odd nostalgia for the rhetoric of the Cold War.

A writer at the *Calgary Herald* wrote a column in late 2002—presumably with tongue in cheek—fondly remembering "Tail-Gunner Joe" McCarthy, the Red-baiting US senator of the early 1950s, and suggesting the creation of a committee on "un-Albertan activities" to deal with everyone on the wrong side of the Kyoto Protocol discussion. An *Edmonton Sun* columnist was sued in the 1990s for calling another journalist a communist. Rod Love, Klein's former chief of staff, started a consulting firm when he left government in 1998. In 1999, he wrote the minister of economic development to complain that "communists" on the town council in Canmore were holding up a $1-billion resort development. He later apologized for his verbal enthusiasm. Klein apologized only when necessary. In the mid-1990s, Klein called Kevin Taft a "communist" for a book on Alberta government policies. The attack helped set Taft on a road that culminated with his becoming provincial Liberal leader in early 2004. At that point, reminded of his earlier jab, Klein said to reporters: "Did I call him that? That was being too kind."

Personal taunts and coarseness were hardly exclusive property in Alberta. The early 1980s had proved that. The notorious bumper sticker, reading: "Let the Eastern Bastards Freeze in the Dark," was one of the milder artifacts of the era. In those days you could drive through the countryside near Three Hills and see a white-haired couple pass by in a big Ford with a bumper sticker reading: Margaret Has One, Trudeau Is One.

Alberta voters who backed Klein and later found themselves on the receiving end of this type of behaviour had no recourse. They had joined in the creation of a virtual one-party state and a government from which there was little appeal. More than just the weakness of the other parties was in play. Talking to people around Alberta during elections turned up a characteristic tendency to view politics as a matter of identity rather than of choice. Especially in rural areas, they often said they would not easily lean Liberal or New Democrat because they were Conservative—not that they *preferred* the Conservative party, but that they *were* Conservative. What happens when you feel abused by the very organization that makes up part of your identity? In Alberta, the result seemed to be a powerful reinforcement of political apathy.

Empty Ballots

About halfway through the 2001 provincial election, Klein strolled through a giant truckstop in Leduc, on Highway 2 just south of Edmonton. The lunchtime crowd in the restaurant took in the aura of a celebrity trailed by TV cameras and gave him a warm reception. Klein walked among the tables, shaking hands, and exchanging a few words. A beefy, middle-aged truck driver sitting with a skinnier companion shook hands with Klein and said he thought the premier was doing a good job. Klein thanked him and moved on. The beefier driver waited until the premier was out of earshot and told his buddy, without a trace of a smile: "He's not as fat as he looks on TV."

The minor surface turbulence of Alberta politics is a deceiving thing. You don't really know what you're dealing with until you dive in and feel the deep, cold, dangerous currents underneath. The coldest and most dangerous is a streak of withdrawal. The Reform party started in 1987 with the slogan "The West Wants In." But in Alberta, the unspoken slogan of a lot of people is "We Don't Care." The trouble is a lot of them do care; they just don't know anymore what they can do about it.

John Davies ran a foundry in Lethbridge. He was an engineer and the president of Lethbridge Iron Works, one of the family-owned businesses that made up the appealing picture of Alberta as a home of smart, willing entrepreneurs. When the province deregulated the electricity market, medium-sized businesses like Lethbridge Iron Works found themselves facing sharply rising prices and a limited, confused marketing structure.

Davies jumped into the public debate over electricity deregulation by writing a critique of the government's plans. His paper was one of the few informed commentaries on a process hardly anyone in the province understood. He began to play a key role for businesses lobbying politicians. He was eventually named to the province's electric power advisory council, created to comment on the issues raised by deregulation. In short, he did everything an aware and concerned citizen ought to be doing.

In May 2003, he was dropped from the advisory council. Energy Minister Murray Smith wrote Davies a letter thanking him for his two years of service. "I had to read between the lines that I wasn't being invited back," Davies told a reporter. Among the new appointees in May 2003 were two Progressive Conservative members of the legislature. Among members reappointed was Don Lowry, president of the city of Edmonton-owned utility Epcor Inc; Lowry had limited his public criticism to a single public comment, and had written a same-day letter of apology after receiving a phone call from Klein's chief of staff, Peter

Elzinga, the morning the comment appeared in a newspaper. Two months later, Davies was linking the government's single-minded course on electricity to the state of political life in the province: "I think if we had an opposition, things would be different. Right now, we barely have a government, they sit for so little time. In Alberta, democracy isn't working and it shows. . . . People are apathetic, and over time, they get used to it."

Voter apathy was causing concern around North America by then. In Alberta, as elsewhere, ordinary people were being told they had a choice between political parties but no real policy choice: globalization and technology meant that local communities could no longer run their own affairs. But, Alberta threw a strange local development into the mix. Apathy here was largely a product of success.

Things seemed to pass a breaking point somewhere around 2000 and 2001. That's when voters normally willing to talk about an election campaign started saying they had given up.

The first overt signs came during the September 2000 by-election in Red Deer to replace Stockwell Day, who had gone on to federal politics. The by-election set a record for political futility. Only one in five of the constituency's approximately 20,000 registered voters showed up. The turnout of 20.4 per cent was the lowest recorded for any by-election in Alberta's history. There had been a handful of acclamations, but the last occurred in 1940. Paul Johnston, a political scientist at the University of Alberta and specialist in voting issues, said immediately afterward that voters stay home when they are satisfied. They also stay home when they are frustrated, he said: "This is very characteristic of one-party dominant states."

The general election next March told much the same story. The campaign gave the Conservatives 62 per cent of the popular vote but nearly 90 per cent (74 out of 83) of seats in the legislature. It was the sort of margin that made Alberta look like a solid, undifferentiated mass on the national stage. Down at street level, the voters added a much rougher texture to the superficially smooth surface of their decision.

In Red Deer, core Progressive Conservative supporters offered classic reasons for re-electing the government. Klein inspires trust, Doug Hazelton, an older man, said at the doorstep of his home: "One of the biggest things I like is he's done away with the biggest part of the debt. He's made mistakes, everybody makes mistakes . . . if there's anybody that's 110-per-cent Albertan, he is." Naomi Cully, a banker, said she liked the government's tax cuts and so did her husband. She was less happy about the way some of the province's spending cuts had affected her husband's job at the local hospital, but her worry about taxes outweighed that: "There's two of us working, and I feel like I'm footing the bill for everybody."

There could hardly have been a better summary of the sources of the government's popularity. But then, there was the convenience store clerk who said of the election, "I don't know anything about it. I don't want to know about it." And, there was the woman who, asked what she wanted to hear from the candidates, replied with a jolly, "Can't think of a darned thing." Every second or third person in the city that February was talking that way.

Otto Pahl from Three Hills, about halfway between Red Deer and Calgary, said he would vote for his local Conservative candidate, who happened to be a friend. But, he added: "I hope the opposition is bigger. It's fine to have a majority government, but it should be just barely a majority."

All along Highway 39, on the road from Leduc to the oilfield and farm country around Drayton Valley, solid Conservative country in the end, bitterness and disappointment roiled underneath a surface layer of firm Conservative support. Michelle Nahuliak, a young office clerk in Thorsby, said she thought anyone would be better than Klein, but: "I don't really believe in voting because, no matter what, Klein is still going to get in." Rick Ayotte said in Drayton Valley that he saw no accountability in any government. He was not planning to vote: "The woman Liberal leader, Nancy (MacBeth), she's full of crap. . . . Ralph Klein, as far as I'm concerned, he sold out as soon as he got into government."

Later that day, Klein appeared at the Elks Club in Drayton Valley and delivered one of the most emotional and persuasive speeches of his career. He cut up MacBeth's campaign with razor wit and spoke of his own dreams to a rapt audience of about 250 people. Most of them were white-haired, dressed in the boots and patterned shirts that denoted local farmers. He did not offer them a promised land of justice and equality, or a future of new departures. He spoke of more mundane hopes that many people shared: "I have the vision of a strong economy. . . . I have a vision of new jobs for our young people, good jobs." And especially, he had a vision of no provincial debt and ever-lower taxes. The key lay not so much in what he said as in his obvious emotional trust in the audience. His habitual wariness gave way to a shared baring of the soul. But, these were the core supporters. Outside, all around the country, lived the disbelievers.

High Wire Act

Voters had new reason to become engaged in politics a couple of years later. People in many parts of Alberta were confused and angry about the results of the January 1, 2001 deregulation of the electricity industry. Household bills were too complicated for many people to read. The promised retail competition did not show up for ordinary households. That failure reflected a predictable split in the marketplace—by early 2004 there were seventeen retailers offering electricity to large commercial and industrial users, five selling to small commercial and industrial customers, and two selling to ordinary households. Most of all, prices had climbed. Electricity deregulation was sold as a means of keeping prices down. Instead, prices went up immediately and the first thing the government did in the "deregulated" market was cap retail prices going into the 2001 election. The old price of less than four cents a kilowatt-hour was apparently gone forever.

Unrest spread to the government's key rural supporters, who confronted several Conservative cabinet ministers at an annual convention of the Alberta Association of Municipal Districts and Counties in 2003. Reinhold Ortlieb, a rancher and county councillor from the Leduc area, just south of Edmonton, said he had paid $451 for power one month early in 2000 and paid $1,400 for one month's supply of electricity two years later: "I'm going down the road broke if this keeps up." Rural areas complained they were looking at having to shut down community halls because of utility bills.

The two men most responsible for completing the push to deregulation eventually pulled back on their promise that it would bring lower prices. Former cabinet minister Steve West said in May 2003 that people would see the benefits in another nine years. Uttering one of his patented sweeping generalizations, unsupported by any documented evidence, he told an interviewer: "It takes ten years for any change to effect itself. By 2012 it will be sorted out." The following winter, Klein conceded that deregulation might never reduce costs for consumers.

Deregulation of electricity was a vastly complicated business. Alberta was one of the best of a bad lot of North American jurisdictions that had jumped into it. Generators were responding with new plants and different technologies. The drawbacks included higher prices and consumer confusion. As a policy decision, deregulation had pros and cons. As an exercise in democratic decision making, it served as a case study in the poverty of Alberta politics. The electricity experiment recycled some of the key recurring features of Alberta's public life:

- Lack of debate: The legislature did not engage in intensive debate of the landmark amendments to the province's electric utilities law in 1996. General public discussion was almost non-existent. Information was in short supply and largely limited to the heavily theoretical report of a US-based firm of consulting economists.

- Suppression of dissent and management of debate: John Davies and Don Lowry were living examples.

- Buying off voters: The bill for various electricity rebates announced before the 2001 election hit $2 billion. The same people inclined to complain about federal vote-buying responded by giving the government the biggest majority it had won in three elections with Ralph Klein as leader.

- Control of local governments: A major complication of electricity restructuring was the presence of large utilities owned by the cities of Calgary and Edmonton. The province relentlessly campaigned to paint the city utilities as bad actors in the marketplace, and to hedge them in with regulations that tended to create pressure on the cities to sell them to private investors.

- Dropping the second shoe: Klein and West conceded that prices would not drop in the short term and might never drop fully to old levels. More important was the gradual admission by power generators that, in the long run, companies building plants would need the ability to sell excess power into the US But that would require construction of a new transmission line worth an estimated $1 billion or more. Some or all the costs would apparently fall on Alberta consumers.

- Foggy accounting: One of the chief arguments for deregulation was that it would allow for more efficient planning and financing of new generating plants. That did not acknowledge why new plants were needed. Households and farms accounted for only one-sixth of electricity needs in the province in 1995, and their demand was not growing by huge amounts. The biggest and fastest growing use was commercial and industrial, much of it related to the oil and gas industry. Deregulation was sold to ordinary householders as a way to keep their prices down; its purpose was to find a new way to provide more power for oil sands plants, gas fields, and other industries.

- Helplessness: Establishing an electricity structure based on market forces did more than remove people's ability to make decisions in common on a necessity of daily life. It denied Alberta consumers the kinds of tools that were popping up even in deregulated markets in the United States. Some states allowed municipalities to bargain for power on behalf of all their residents. US municipalities like Jacksonville, Florida, remained key players in the electricity business. The new electricity market ruled out the lingering Alberta traditions of self-help expressed in organizations such as livestock feeder associations, which were backstopped by government guarantees.

Hearing Voices

As with the shift to a flat-rate provincial income tax, no one directly asked Alberta voters whether they wanted to push ahead with a new electricity market structure. Policy often arose from the combination of ideology, private consultation with experts, and an entrenched government.

Control of public discourse spread into newspapers as well. The prevailing method of political journalism in the province drifted toward a deliberate strategy of getting along with the government in exchange for a steady diet of leaks that led to "exclusive" stories—stories usually about inconsequential matters or full of inaccuracies.

What to make of this? The most rational explanation was that many Alberta voters were putting their trust in Klein personally. Yet, there were reasons to wonder. A survey done by the University of Alberta's Population Research Laboratory in 2003 for the Parkland Institute found only 40 per cent of the province saying that democracy was "healthy" or "very healthy" in Alberta.

The Progressive Conservative party not only dominated provincial politics, it kept getting stronger than its rivals. In 2003, it collected $2.3 million in donations. By the spring of 2004, it had $4.17 million on hand. That was enough to pay for two election campaigns, and fundraising for the coming election had not yet started. The Liberals had official Opposition status, a $900,000 debt and had raised $348,759 the preceding year. The New Democrats had two MLAs and had raised $417,966.

"How does the opposition get its message out?" Keith Brownsey, a political scientist at Mount Royal College, commented. "Ralph Klein has all the money." He also had much of the top political talent on his team. For anyone in opposition, the notion of Alberta politics as a study in poverty had all too literal a meaning.

Alberta has had to contend with a double-sided populism. Many people here tend to think of politics as a struggle to maintain control by the "grassroots," the ordinary voters Klein took to calling "severely normal Albertans." But who was a "severely normal Albertan?"

The half-dozen people who wrote Klein in January 2001 proposing a "firewall" around Alberta to protect it from the federal government were severely abnormal Albertans. They consisted of academics, policy analysts, and would-be political leaders. Yet they received immediate credibility in the form of heavy media attention, including a story and a posed, front-page portrait in the *National Post*. The working assumption in the media is that anything claiming to represent western alienation is important, genuine, and deeply rooted in the population at large because—well, because the West is defined partly as a place that is always alienated. It is a case of self-replication, with each copy a little more faded and less true to life.

Far below the public awareness radar lay the mundane reality of many other Albertans. A few days before the "firewall" letter was sent in a blaze of publicity to Klein's office, a woman wrote to Gary Severtson, Progressive Conservative member of the legislature for Innisfail, asking about the outrageous treatment her ninety-one-year-old father had received in the weeks before his recent death. She said he was kept in a chair or wheelchair all day rather than being allowed to nap in his room in a nursing home. He had to wait in his bed until ten AM for breakfast. In hospital once, he had been given a laxative, then left unattended in a chair; his aged wife was telephoned later and told to come get his laundry. Finally: "The night before he died he was the last to leave the dining room, even though he was suffering from pneumonia."

This was a real voice from real Alberta. Somehow it did not carry as far as the theories of a handful of Calgary policy analysts who claimed what real Albertans really wanted was their own provincial police force and new provincial bureaucracies to run separate tax and pension plans.

Definitions and jostling for public attention are only part of the dilemma, however. The ordinary "grassroots" who want control can in fact be a minority. The paradoxical demand for political power for minorities has been evident for some time in federal affairs. The public call for the 1987 "western assembly" in Vancouver, which led to creation of the Reform party, raised the spectre that "half of English-speaking Canada will live in metro Toronto by the year 2000." It demanded institutional change such as Senate reform that "compels the government to meet the interests of the less populous areas."

Less apparent is the nature of this phenomenon inside Alberta. The dominant single party functions in part as the tool to protect "the interests of the less populous areas" in Alberta, usually the more rural areas. Protecting those interests has a long tradition. The United Farmers of Alberta—the province's first expression of distrust of the political process—came to power in 1921 with 28.9 per cent of the popular vote compared with 34 per cent for the Liberals; the UFA's votes were spread more effectively around rural areas of the province and resulted in election of more members of the legislature. The UFA stayed in power until 1935 despite never gaining more than 39.7 per cent of the popular vote.

These numbers aren't feasible anymore. Now, the rural regions have to throw in their lot with a dominant party. The strategy often works, but it is also a trap. Committed to the strategy of government by a single dominant party, voters trying to protect what power they have also find themselves committed to maintaining a perpetually weak democracy. When it does not meet their needs, they have nowhere else to turn.

RURAL ALBERTA AND POLITICAL MONO-CULTURE

The poverty of Alberta politics deepens the further you go into the mythical home of western virtues in rural Alberta. The countryside is supposed to be rich in democratic tradition. In some ways it still is. Yet, rural Alberta has become increasingly threadbare in its political options.

When rural ridings vote by 70-per-cent margins for the federal Conservative party, they are seen as expressing the ultimate word in western alienation. Their anger can have genuine sources. For people in the countryside, the federal gun registry really is a huge waste of money and a sign of disrespect for local culture. Their culture is eroding in deeper ways, however. Their economy is under perennial threat. And, their political alienation begins at home, with the realization they are trapped inside the boundaries of a virtual one-party state, boundaries whose stakes they have helped set in the ground.

The end point is resignation: "I don't really believe in voting because, no matter what, Klein is still going to get in." Anyone still looking for a way out gets stuck in confusion and frustration.

No Exit

You could see the gates close at small events—like a meeting one night in the winter of 2000 in Stettler, population about 5,000, an oilfield service and agricultural centre poised on the invisible dividing line where the relative lushness of central Alberta gives way with surprising suddenness to the sparser pastures and grain fields of the dry southeast. It was a nippy Monday night, but there were people downtown. Customers sat in restaurants talking away the evening and looking out into the February darkness. Inside the Legion hall a handful of people drank slow beers and played shuffleboard. The rocks slid perfectly down the slick, waxed surface. You wouldn't want to walk in and start a casual game with one of the regulars.

Through a back door, down a hall, stood another door, framed by a folk-art depiction of the bloody Canadian landing at Dieppe in 1942. The past keeps its hold here. On the other side of that door a surprising crowd was gathering. About sixty people showed up for a meeting arranged by the Friends of Medicare. The organization was city-based, but someone had found it on the Internet and started a local chapter here in Stettler. The people in the crowd were worried about the provincial government's talk of contracting out major surgery to privately owned clinics. Only four of five of them looked to be under retirement age. These were the classic bedrock supporters of the Progressive Conservative party in small towns across the province. But on this night they were listening to another senior, Dr. Harold Swanson, a Calgary physician who had become so upset about the Alberta government's health policy that he had run for the Liberals against Ralph Klein in the 1997 election.

The complaints about Klein's lack of a plan for the health system were wrong, Swanson told them. "In my view, he did have a plan—one to commercialize, Americanize, corporatize our public health-care structure." Contracting out surgery had been tried, and it had failed, he said. "It is not innovative or new, having previously been tried in other countries." It allows extra-billing by doctors under another name, he said. The questions after his twenty-minute speech indicated worry. Where did doctors stand on private surgery? If Klein signed twenty-year contracts would they remain in effect after he retired? Was there any chance of a referendum on this issue? How could health care be fixed? At the back, not quite believing what she was seeing and hearing, sat Sandra Rairdan, recently retired chairwoman of the provincially appointed East Central Health Authority. These folks should realize that it's time to get on with the job, she commented later.

After an hour of talk, most of the audience picked up information pamphlets and cards telling them how to get in touch with members of the legislature. Yet, they left with their past in tow. These were the people who had spent the last half-century accepting one-party politics as the Alberta way. Would fear and uncertainty push the aging Friends of Medicare in Stettler to vote for another party, even if voting for another party was the only political lever they had? It would mean changing their sense of who they were. It would be nearly as big a change as deciding they no longer belonged in the Legion Hall, with its comfortable community rituals and the home-created mural of a long-ago, faraway battle that changed some families' lives forever. They had spent most of a lifetime agreeing, "Who else is there to vote for?" Hemmed in by their own past, where would they turn?

The closing in of rural Alberta's political life was on display again a few months later in the smaller community of Alix, located partway between Stettler and Lacombe. About 400 people gathered on a blustery, chilly June night at the

Alix hockey arena to decide on a Progressive Conservative candidate for the provincial constituency of Lacombe-Stettler. The campaign had begun in March. It had proved unexpectedly gruelling but was ending in a civilized setting. Faded wooden arena signs posted to govern behaviour at decades of local hockey games warned all who entered: Swearing, Spitting, Fighting Prohibited.

Judy Gordon, a two-term member of the legislature from Lacombe, was trying to hang on to the nomination against Jack Hayden, a farmer from the Stettler area in the southeast corner of the constituency and president of the Alberta Association of Municipal Districts and Counties. Both were down-to-earth individuals grounded in local politics.

Yet, their home bases were different. Lacombe, home to about 10,000 people, lay just off Highway 2, the paved corridor between Edmonton and Calgary. It was drifting into that urban axis, and its commercial life was geared partly to visiting city dwellers. Stettler had nearly 5,000 fewer people and a less diversified local economy. There was more going on here than the usual town rivalry that creates tension in just about every rural constituency in the province. Hayden based his campaign specifically on strengthening the voice of agriculture in the government. "I'm used to going in and making a good case for rural communities," he said. Gordon countered with promises of farm help and said she was pushing to locate a renal dialysis centre in Stettler. Gordon won. Hayden's people left the rink quietly. Fred Mueller from the nearby town of Joffre told a crestfallen Hayden the result might be for the best: "You can probably do more for us right where you are. You can go to ministers and . . . call a spade a spade."

In later years, Hayden often found himself doing exactly that. More and more, the rural communities that provided the backbone of the Conservative government's political support were protesting the effects of the government's beliefs in centralized power and in deregulation of what had been public utilities. By 2003, small communities around the province were worried that soaring prices in the province's newly deregulated electricity market were crushing the budgets for local halls, curling rinks, and hockey arenas. Counties were being asked for grant money to help pay power bills that had roughly tripled—typically from a range of $4,000 or $5,000 to $12,000 or $15,000 a year. Local administrators wondered what would happen to their community life. "There are all kinds of implications here," Hayden said. "Rural Albertans, quite frankly, are not feeling the Alberta Advantage like they should."

In the spring of 2004, Hayden was dealing with the regulation of intensive livestock operations. Two years earlier, the government had passed a law transferring regulation of large confined feeding operations from municipalities to the provincially appointed Natural Resources Conservation Board. The transfer of authority ended a budding series of mini-civil wars that pitted growing farm operations against reluctant rural neighbours around Alberta. It cleared the way for more livestock industry expansion that was a key in the government's rural economic strategies. It also removed important local authority over land use, as Hayden pointed out. Now his association was complaining that a new bill— quickly pushed through the legislature—had further eroded the authority of municipalities. Hayden said the new law made Alberta the only province in the country in which municipalities did not control the location of so-called factory farms. "We are moving into the area where the municipalities will not be able to determine land use," he said. "For the most part, we feel we were completely ignored."

His language mirrored the language usually seen as expressing western alienation—a protest against a central government ignoring the wishes of local residents and overriding local governments. But, Hayden's protests indicated an alienation felt and expressed on a different plane. The blowups over electricity policy and regulation of the livestock industry were not the result of regional tension. They were not even a result of urban-rural differences. The reality was that many neighbouring farmers led protests against giant pig barns and cattle feedlots that were often seen as manure factories. In 2002, the Natural Resources Conservation Board answered 981 complaints about 431 livestock operations around the province. They weren't all coming from dilettante urban acreage owners. Inspectors issued 36 enforcement orders and had warned another 122 operators. What was going on here?

A Shrinking World

It is too easy and simplistic to write off "western alienation" as a rural phenomenon. But, what is called western alienation often springs from rural discontent. And, that discontent springs from a complex network of fears: of economic disaster, of cultural loss, of the loss of political influence not just in Canada but within provincial borders, especially in the rapidly urbanizing province of Alberta.

The central question for understanding the politics of discontent in rural Alberta is why the discontent should be pictured as "western." Why is it a reaction against Ottawa or Central Canada and not against the provincial government or Edmonton or Calgary?

There are immediately visible answers. Regional protest builds on a long tradition and has become an automatic pathway for political action. The Alberta government delivers enough benefits to rural residents that any complaints are outweighed. In contrast, the federal presence has tended to be withdrawn (for example with the abolition of the Crowsnest rail freight rates), or beaten back by the province (for example, with the Alberta government's decades of effort to undermine the Canadian Wheat Board). And, it is easier to affect provincial decisions than federal decisions; provincial politicians are more accessible.

Some less apparent answers may carry equal or even heavier weight. If a way of life is disappearing, it may be easier to continue a futile game of protest against Central Canada than to face up to reality by dealing with issues at home. To say you have lost a political debate to Ontario is one thing; you still have a regional identity to fall back on, and you can still try to shift the issue into provincial jurisdiction to change the outcome. Saying you have lost a debate to other Albertans is quite another thing: there are no alternatives left; you have to think of yourself as part of an anonymous losing minority rather than as an Albertan or westerner.

That has meant getting boxed into a political dead end—replacing political debate with trust in a strong leader and participation in a dominant political party from which there is no appeal. The supposed "mavericks" gather into a tame herd because the alternative is isolation. And, they have a huge incentive: Alberta is the one province in the West where rural leaders have preserved an improbably large role in government.

The "politics of anti-politics" represents a streak of Alberta life that goes back to the 1920s and was renewed in the 1990s. In rural Alberta it covers up a critical tension. The same people who want to get rid of politics also want to make sure that some useful political institutions exist, and that those institutions will be run by their own representatives.

There's a constant clash here between anti-politics and a quest for the preservation of political power. It showed up vividly during hearings in 1995 on how to redraw provincial political boundaries. There was significant talk at the time about reducing the number of seats in the legislature and about trying harder to make sure that each constituency had more or less the same population. Both changes would have reduced the rural presence in the legislature.

This was taking place at the peak of the first wave of the Klein Revolution—a period in which government was supposed to be cut down to size and decisions made on the basis of marketplace realities. The superficial principles were tossed out the window when rural political power came into question.

The boundary commissioners travelled to the east-central town of St. Paul, where they heard Mike Hermansen, from the nearby community of Breton, argue there would be nothing wrong with letting rural constituencies have 25 per cent fewer people in them than urban constituencies. He offered a specific reason why rural and urban voters should not be counted equally: "We believe that rural concerns would not be given priority."

Paul Langevin, the local member of the legislature, explained that the province needed many rural MLAs like him because he had to deal with a variety of local interests: school boards, local officials looking for provincial grants, independent loggers looking for sources of timber, and operators of about thirty or forty traplines. The government had vigorously been trying to reduce the number of local authorities, but one of its MLAs protested that representing them was central to his job. "It's part of the tradition," Langevin concluded.

Brian Stecyk, representative of a Progressive Conservative constituency association and editor of the party's provincial newsletter, also made the case for keeping many rural constituencies with small populations. "Being fair does not have to mean being equal," he said. That one-sentence plea captured the emotional core of decades of political sentiment across an entire region. At bottom, it's a call to give a minority more than its share of political power in order to meet its view of fairness.

Alberta politics are unique in this way. Alberta is the last place in the West where rural residents can feel they occupy that unequal—but in their view necessary and traditional—share of political power. Cities have come to dominate governments in Manitoba and Saskatchewan. It is in more heavily urbanized Alberta that rural politicians have paradoxically been able to maintain the biggest role in the provincial government.

Much of the province's reaction against federal power has reflected this attempt to hang on to a level of influence no longer justified by population numbers.

The Reform party was founded in 1987 largely as a rural-centred protest movement. Party leader Preston Manning built and solidified his support by the venerable tactic of face-to-face contact with ordinary people in small communities. For years he made regular appearances around rural Alberta—articulating what was on people's minds in high-pitched, carefully measured tones or listening owl-eyed behind his glasses as they tried to express for themselves what was bothering them. It was after he succumbed to the call of national politics, and the rhetoric of television, that he lost the leadership of what had become the Alliance party to Stockwell Day.

Even the desultory push for Senate reform produced a little noticed variation on the theme of preserving an outsized rural presence. Alberta's position going into constitutional negotiations in 1992 was that each province should be able to decide whether to elect senators to represent the entire province or to represent constituencies to be created within each province. Alberta's minister of federal affairs favoured drawing up constituencies; the effect would have been to reserve a number of Senate seats for rural representatives. He also wanted a fairly large number of senators, which would have enhanced the effect; the greater the number of senators, the more room for rural senators.

But, rural influence comes at an extremely heavy price: acceptance that the province's political life is run by a single, dominant party. At one point before the 2001 provincial election, Liberal agriculture critic Ken Nicol saw a growing unease around parts of the Alberta countryside. Too obviously for Nicol's comfort, they were not searching for a Liberal alternative. He took to suggesting that they consider an option like forming an Alberta version of the Saskatchewan Party. "I don't go out and promote it," he said. "I don't want to destroy the Liberal opportunities. . . . But when it comes down to it and they say, 'Look, we don't feel comfortable supporting the Liberals,' then I tell them, 'Look, this is an option.'"

Nicol's idea was that a big enough contingent of legislators from a rural-based third party could hold the balance of power between Liberals and Conservatives. That would work only if a third party could be organized, and only if the Liberals could survive as a sizable opposition. Sticking with the Conservatives posed some problems but put a rural politician at much smaller risk. The reward for that risk was huge.

It came with an implied trade-off. People in rural Alberta got influence. What they gave in return was not only election support, but a sort of moral authority. They provided a salt-of-the-earth cover for urban ideologues who might otherwise find themselves not only making a tough sell but pictured as a minority elite. The damaging result for rural Albertans was that some of their urban partners kept pressing for a "conservatism" based on free play of market forces; that was sometimes the opposite of rural Alberta's vision of "conservatism."

There was an important distinction to keep in mind here. Rural Alberta no longer meant the same as agricultural Alberta. A rural Albertan was more likely to drive an oilfield service truck, or run a florist shop, or handle tax returns than to run a farm. If rural dwellers felt a kinship with farmers it was a literal family relationship or a recognition that some of their income was based on local farm income. The number of active, full-time farmers in Alberta had fallen to about 3 per cent of the population by the 1990s. But, farm owners generally made up at least one-quarter of the legislative assembly. That was their last grip on any sort of formal political power. The question was what good could it do them?

Survival

In late 2003, Ralph Klein provoked a few days of headlines with a vague reference to western separatism as a remedy for Alberta's displeasure with Ottawa, or more accurately as a remedy for his government's displeasure with the federal government.

Media organizations went along with the gag. Western alienation was a guaranteed, ready-made story, just like the daily ups and downs of the stock market or any random facts that could be grouped around the phrase "baby boomers."

A funny little fact escaped attention during the brief period before Klein pulled back, claiming he had been misinterpreted. The only time a political party representing itself as even quasi-separatist ever made a big impact in Alberta was in 1982, and that eruption was a challenge not to the federal government but to the provincial Progressive Conservatives.

The Western Canada Concept party sprang out of nowhere to win a by-election in southern Alberta in the spring of 1982. It was wiped out in a general election that fall, but it did manage to put a scare into Premier Peter Lougheed and his governing party. It garnered about one-eighth of the popular vote, primarily in rural areas. Then it disappeared. Gord Kesler, the sometime rodeo rider and oilfield scout who had become for a few months a WCC member of the legislature, disappeared just as effectively. By the late 1990s, a distant relative in the town of Olds could say only that he thought the man who had briefly stirred up Alberta politics had moved to the United States, but he could not be sure about that.

The next two decades would bring Alberta farmers a never-ending string of problems and outright disasters—continued high interest rates; wobbly or sinking grain prices; consolidation of farms that in some cases saw extended families owning more than a township of land; off-and-on droughts; sagging pork prices; and mad cow disease. Alberta came out of this period with damage but measurably better off than either Saskatchewan or Manitoba. Intensive irrigation farming in the south was producing profits. Cattle prices picked up in the 1990s, injecting large amounts of cash into a provincial farm economy heavily geared toward livestock. A resurgent natural gas industry provided cash for leases of surface access. A generally booming economy provided income through the second jobs that many farm families had come to accept as normal.

There were still huge concerns. Farming was becoming more and more concentrated in fewer hands. In early 2004, representatives of Alberta Pork, representing the province's pig farmers, told a committee of government MLAs their organization was down to 1,514 producer-members, a drop of 241 from the preceding year. They said the province had about 4,000 pig producers in 1996 and about 26,000 in 1971. This drastically shrunken base of farmers ran operations so large they were raising about 15 million pigs a year, 15 per cent of Canadian production. Bigger farms meant shrinking or disappearing communities.

Intermittent disasters translated into calls for government help. This went against the grain of both myth and the personal inclinations of many people, but it seemed inescapable. The Alberta government spent hundreds of millions of dollars in the late 1980s propping up farmers through interest-rate subsidies and other programs. The full cost was never measured because a lot of it did not show up as a program expense. Some ended up recorded as deficits of hundreds of millions of dollars on the books of provincial corporations providing loans or insurance.

When Don Getty came under attack from within his own Conservative party in the early 1990s, widespread complaints about budget deficits focused on multimillion-dollar business loans and ignored the massive spending that had shored up a faltering rural economy. The Klein-era governments had a respite during a period of strong cattle prices but eventually handed out hundreds of millions of dollars in drought assistance in the early 2000s and in aid during the BSE crisis.

The steady flow of money could not overcome a persistent dread. There is a standard connection made in commentaries on Alberta politics. Western alienation is usually linked to the boom-and-bust nature of the province's resource-based economy. What goes missing in this interpretation is an acknowledgement that the energy industry has been far more stable than agriculture.

The annual economic accounts for Alberta show ups and downs in a variety of industries. They confirm the investment collapse of 1982, which began in oil and gas, and the effects of the oil price collapse of 1986.

But, nothing swings up and down like farm revenue. In a really tough or really good year, corporation profits in Alberta can swing by 30 or 40 per cent. Income in most other sectors of the economy rarely changes by more than 15 per cent in a given year. But the accrued net income of farm operators (cash receipts plus inventory changes) swings wildly from year to year with no reference to the surrounding economy—down 61 per cent in 1991, up 221 per cent in 1992, down 76 per cent in 1994, up 502 per cent in 1995, down 95 per cent in 2002 (the year that new talk of separatism and firewalls started setting in). Farm cash receipts in Alberta fell another 15.6 per cent in 2003 during the BSE crisis.

Lurches on this scale translate into a never-ending quest for security. Only governments are able to provide the desired security. But, governments run by outsiders are never fully trusted. In the 1990s the situation grew worse. The ability of any government to counteract global economic trends—even the desirability of a government trying to do so—fell into serious question.

For rural Alberta this meant living with a never-ending mental conflict. The preferred model of government was captured by one of the Klein-era government's widely promoted catch-phrases: staying "out of the business of business." But, economic reality meant that rural Alberta wanted the government very much involved in rural business. It wanted the province to provide financial and infrastructure support. It wanted a seemingly endless string of aid programs for specific disasters.

The Progressive Conservatives under Ralph Klein basically amounted to a double coalition. Klein fused the "Red Tory" remnants of the federal Progressive Conservatives with the breakaway elements that formed the Reform party. He also bridged the gap between urban Alberta (primarily Calgary) and rural Alberta. His government was able to do that because it could afford the required spending. In Saskatchewan, highways and hospitals disappeared under financial pressure, and so did the New Democrat government's ability to elect members in just about any rural constituency.

The cross-border comparison suggests one reason why in many opinion surveys, Saskatchewan scores highest on items that might be taken as related to western alienation. In a number of ways, Saskatchewan turns out to be more like the stereotypical image of Alberta than Alberta is. The numbers are a little soft because the findings for individual provinces in national polls typically carry a margin of error in the range of 7 or 8 per cent, but the pattern of stronger opinions in Saskatchewan is firm.

The Alberta government strongly opposed creation of a national health council. An Ipsos-Reid poll in May 2003 found 56 per cent of people in Alberta saying they would be more likely to vote for a member of the provincial legislature who opposed the creation of a national health council, but 74 per cent agreeing in Saskatchewan and Manitoba (sometimes surveyed as a combined region for statistical purposes). Asked if the federal government would be right to create a national health council despite resistance from some provinces, 48 per cent of those asked in Alberta said yes and 42 per cent in Saskatchewan and Manitoba.

In January 2004, Ipsos-Reid asked whether Canada should get rid of the federal gun registry. There was strong agreement from 44 per cent of people asked in Alberta and 52 per cent in Saskatchewan and Manitoba. In Alberta, 42 per cent strongly or somewhat disagreed and in Manitoba and Saskatchewan, 37 per cent strongly or somewhat disagreed.

At the end of March 2004, Ipsos-Reid asked whether Canada's health system should exclude corporations operating for profit and instead rely solely with public and non-profit health-care providers. In Alberta, 38 per cent of people strongly agreed and 27 per cent somewhat agreed. In the Saskatchewan–Manitoba region, 25 per cent strongly agreed and 24 per cent somewhat agreed.

Asked at the same time whether infrastructure such as hospitals, schools, highways, and water systems should be developed through direct public investment and not through joint ventures with corporations, 35 per cent of people contacted in Alberta agreed and 37 per cent somewhat agreed. In Saskatchewan and Manitoba, 29 per cent strongly agreed and 35 per cent somewhat agreed. The free-market leanings were slightly stronger across the border than in supposedly rugged, anti-government Alberta, where the provincial government was making public-private joint ventures a major priority.

Various surveys by the Canada West Foundation have found measures of alienation highest in Saskatchewan. No one has looked closely at why these differences exist. They may reflect the more urbanized, slightly more cosmopolitan nature of Alberta life. It is also possible that people in Saskatchewan, tied more to agriculture and with a less diversified agricultural economy, feel a level of economic insecurity that gets expressed in its political opinions. Rural incomes from all sources in Alberta in 2000 averaged $49,387, more than $8,000 (20 per cent) higher than average rural incomes in Saskatchewan.

Still, the compensation of a bigger irrigation and livestock component in Alberta agriculture does not produce stability. Boom and bust make up the psychology of Alberta's relationship with the economy. No amount of prosperity can ever remove the fear of poverty.

The deeply set nature of this thinking ended up in advertisements for the May 1987 assembly in Vancouver that led later that year to the formation of the Reform party. The headline on the ad read "What does the West want, anyway?" The answers began with economic change: "Our central economic problem is this: all resource industries are subject to violent boom-bust cycles. Nearly all are now in recession, which explains our condition."

The booms and busts were often seen as related to oil and gas prices. That industry did see spectacular growth in the late 1970s. It crashed just as spectacularly in the 1980s, bringing the construction industry down with it in a number of bumps that ended with the oil price collapse of 1986. But, the energy industry goes through longer and more stable cycles. Nothing compares with the violent ups and downs of farm income. The only escape is to sell out and move to a smaller operation or into another way of life.

What is the political effect? A combination of government dependence and surly anti-government sentiment.

Western Conflict

On the one hand, rural Alberta and much of the rural West want government out of their lives, the federal gun registry being a prime example.

On the other hand, they see governments abandoning them. There have been running complaints for years about the perceived ineffectiveness of government crop insurance and income stabilization plans. Corporate control of grain seed and canola seed, and of chemicals, has been spreading, free of the kind of government influence that might have been usual half a century earlier. Alberta's deregulation of the electricity market led to rural anger. Government services have been slipping, although nothing in Alberta has been as emphatic a symbol of that perceived abandonment as the loss of hospitals and crumbling of high-ways in Saskatchewan.

Alberta has been in a special position here as the one government in western Canada most able to afford some continued aid to rural regions. In the fiscal year 2003–04 alone, the province put $776 million into disaster payments to offset the effects of the US border being closed to many cuts of beef and to live cattle as a result of BSE being discovered in an Alberta cow. Drought aid in the immediately preceding years absorbed hundreds of millions more.

And then, there are the scores of everyday items that absorb rural members of the legislature: the small lottery grants for community projects; the tax exemptions for farm fuel (notoriously a privilege that is poorly policed); the never-ending struggle for money to build highways and schools or to refurbish a local hospital; the programs that pay for small towns to hire students for summer jobs; and the continued operation of the Alberta Opportunity Co., a government corporation that has lent money to hundreds of small-town businesses.

What became known as the Klein Revolution amounted in large part to a civil war over who would share the benefits of government aid in a period when the province's ability to shelter people from global market forces was dwindling. In raw terms, people who saw their incomes slipping and hopes for their children fading wanted the government to stop spending money on unionized public-sector work-ers, retired politicians on pension, and businesses lining up for multimillion-dollar loans. They wanted any government spending to go to the people they felt were facing the toughest economic environment.

The conflict between the myth of independence and the reality of clienthood emerged in the root event of the Klein Revolution—the election of Klein as Progressive Conservative party leader in 1992. David Stewart's and Keith Archer's landmark study of voters in that leadership election, published in their book *Quasi-Democracy?*, found that Klein's support had two bases. He won over voters with "populist" attitudes centred on belief in grassroots power and hostility to reg-ulation, but his supporters also favoured universal social programs and the princi-ple that governments should help individuals who had been hit by bad breaks. They favoured that government presence significantly more than supporters of the other leadership candidates.

In Alberta, access to government support means being onside with the gov-erning party. And the longer the governing party stays in power, the more firmly anyone interested in influencing it has to be onside. It is a self-reinforcing mechanism that gets stronger over time.

In federal politics, the same calculation produces an opposite outcome. The constant search for a political party that will reflect and help the local community has ended with a commitment to western-based parties, which in turn means Alberta-based parties. But the more closely any alternative appears to represent only one province, the less likely it is to succeed in a national election. The result is another self-reinforcing cycle leading to a bitter conclusion that Alberta never gets its way.

No Luck

Even the most popular politicians can run into resentment. Premier Ralph Klein ruffled a few feathers early in 2004 by grumpily commenting, in the face of a continuing problem with mad cow disease, that there seemed to be no end to the amount of aid farmers would ask of the provincial government.

Rural Alberta looks at the outside world as a source of economic opportunities and exploits those opportunities with ingenuity and energy. It also sees itself besieged. The pressure squeezes in on everything from ideas for more economically efficient delivery of health care to the prospect for individual landowners in an age of economic globalization. One old farmer from northern Alberta said in early 2000: "These are the only people that are going to be left—Monsanto, Cargill, and IBM." He was a traditional Conservative supporter, not a New Democrat.

The federal gun registry was not the only incursion of a bureaucratized world bothering a lot of people in Alberta. This other populism had no real political outlet. Individuals trying to assert themselves in a world of rules and organizations fought the gun registry or engaged in more reckless acts of rebellion such as refusing to buckle up seat belts. But, their attempts to assert themselves got swept up in Alberta's one-party politics and in the one-dimensional propaganda of "western alienation."

Two decades earlier, western alienation had a different source. Its most vivid expression was anger over the 1980 National Energy Program. All through the small main streets of Alberta's towns and villages, however, other forces were at play. If you had travelled through rural Alberta in the spring of 1982, when heads were being turned by the sudden appearance of the Western Canada Concept party, you would have seen the trailing edges of an older world. It was a world where couples in their 80s would pull out scrapbooks and show mementoes of what life had been like when farming in their area was just getting going in the 1920s. It was a world where a burly, white-haired man who stopped for a sidewalk conversation could recall coming to Alberta as a child by crossing a still open prairie in a horse-drawn wagon that his father drove from North Dakota.

It was a world where the remnants of William Aberhart's and Ernest Manning's Bible Belt still survived. Every town had shops with small posters in their windows advertising evangelical meetings. If you hit a place on the right day, you could attend a lecture at which wide-eyed and flummoxed local men were told that the Bolsheviks had infiltrated Canada's civil service in the 1920s, and the line of their influence could be traced through Lester Pearson down to Pierre Trudeau.

But most of all, it was a world with a sense of impending loss. These were not just people who had seen their financial dreams crashing in the 1980s, although one man in a Taber beer parlour pulled his latest bank receipt out of his pocket to show a reporter that his balance was down to nine cents. They were people who suddenly had to cope with seeing all sorts of public signs in French and thinking their children would have no chance of a job in Ottawa because French was not a language you could easily learn here. They were people whose lives were ordered on the grids set out in regular patterns of 160 acres and of square miles that had suddenly turned into metric fractions because someone in Ottawa had had a bright idea. Some of them still mourned the loss of the Canadian ensign flag.

They were losing, it seemed, everything that had made their lives certain and safe. That has been the rural condition in the West. It creates a separate set of political attitudes.

SECRET FEDERALISTS

If Albertans sometimes sound as if they are fed up with Canada it's usually because they believe in the country strongly and are disappointed with the way it falls short of their dreams.

Back in 1991, a committee of legislators travelled the province to gather ordinary people's views on what should go into the next round of constitutional negotiations. In their report, they took special note of what they'd heard from Buck Kallen of Wainwright, out in the ranch country of east-central Alberta: "With all my heart I beg my leaders to leave no stone unturned, no point undiscussed, no decent idea . . . unconsidered on the path to unity for this country. This is the most unique and beautiful country on the face of the Earth."

Some people here never had much hope for the country. But mostly, the "alienated" sector of Alberta has had a lot of hopes and seen them dashed. They believe in equality and see Quebec and the French language accorded what they regard as a privileged place. They think the federal government can and should help them when they are in trouble, but doubt regional farm disasters ever qualify for as much assistance as something like an ice storm in Central Canada. They want an ethical and efficient government; they get a $1-billion gun registry and a sponsorship scandal. They want their voices to count but see themselves outvoted by Ontario. They want financial security (or outright wealth) in a province full of economic ups and downs and see a National Energy Program intended to move energy exploration to other regions.

Grievance makes a hard road, however. It has been a long time since the NEP was announced in October 1980 and almost as long since Brian Mulroney's government buried it a few years later. That is not to say some people don't have long memories. In the early 1980s, a legislator from southern Alberta complained that the province would never get a fair shake from Ottawa. His evidence was a giant wheat sale to Britain in the late 1940s; he didn't like the terms and was still riled about it. Looking around Alberta these days, you have to wonder what there is to complain about. Many of the real problems are self-inflicted: road deaths, drug abuse, teenage pregnancies, single parenthood, crumbling roads, a political culture sinking into apathy.

Well, there's always a lot to complain about. But, Alberta is not a strange place defined by "western alienation." It is a place a lot like the rest of Canada, populated in large part by people who came here from other provinces. Regional grievance is a specialty crop exploited by shrewd politicians, made to look bigger than it is by unthinking news coverage, and carefully nurtured by a class of professional westerners in the political parties, media, and academic circles.

Never Trust Politicians

If you really don't like a one-party state you can leave. If you want to improve it, one of the ways of going about that is to balance it with another government.

Government members on the 1991 legislature committee on constitutional reform tried hard to bend discussion at public hearings toward recommendations for more provincial power. They ran into resistance. They also received results of a detailed poll that found the majority of people in Alberta leaning toward a federal-provincial sharing of power. Committee member and cabinet minister Dennis Anderson wrote a confidential memo to Premier Don Getty about what he had heard. The analysis was made public when Getty's archives were released to public view more than a decade later.

"Premier," Anderson wrote on June 3, 1991, "there were several surprises during the public hearings . . . if the hearings were at all representative of the views of Albertans, it would seem apparent that there is much more support for a strong federal government than would have been anticipated."

Among what Anderson termed the "less expected results" were: "Absolute support for current national health-care directions, and the national government's involvement in those directions. Support for national education standards. It is less clear that they must be established by the federal government. Relatively strong support for environmental standards to be established federally. Considerable support for federal involvement in all social programs."

That was in the middle of the rise of the Reform party, and its protest agenda highlighted by the slogan "The West Wants In." The persistent and occasionally raucous campaigns by the Alberta government and some of its supporters over the next several years to get the federal government progressively out of the province's life weren't really a reflection of public will; they were part of a prolonged attempt to reshape the public will.

You don't want to go too far here. Even in 1991, most people clearly preferred that provincial governments deliver the programs in many areas. The point was that most Alberta voters did not want either level of government having full and final say over standards and policy decisions in areas like health and education. They wanted a balance and still do. When the Federation of Canadian Municipalities met in Edmonton in 2004, Prime Minister Paul Martin gave hundreds of delegates a new view of the role of cities in Canada: "As we work to improve the places we live, we must never forget that our major cities are this nation's key generation points for economic progress. . . . A New Deal for Canada's cities and communities means that a Liberal government will recognize municipal governments as partners in implementing Canada's national agenda."

A number of the FCM delegates were unimpressed, noting that Martin was starting an election campaign and doubting that a Liberal government could be trusted. But many were happy, believing the new vision of a federal-municipal partnership would put pressure on the province to step in and participate. The Alberta government was not inclined to put cities at the forefront of economic planning. Nor was it inclined to let the federal government roam freely in building partnerships with cities. Ordinary voters, however, seemed as happy about federal intervention in cities as municipal councillors were.

A Compas poll done a week before the FCM meeting in Edmonton found people in Alberta just as willing to see federal support for municipalities as people in other provinces. For example, 39 per cent of Alberta respondents in the poll strongly agreed with federal help for upgrade of municipal roads and 31 per cent somewhat agreed. Willingness to see federal help in fighting crime and preventing terrorism stood a few percentage points higher. Alberta scored the highest of any region in Canada (81 per cent, compared with an overall 75 per cent across Canada) in the number of people agreeing with the statement: "Some people believe that the federal government should assist cities and municipalities because they have real needs and the constitution allows the federal government to spend money wherever it wants."

An Ipsos-Reid poll in July 2004 found a statistical dead heat when people in Alberta were asked whether they favoured Klein's approach to health reform or Martin's (43 per cent for Klein, 39 per cent for Martin with a margin of error of 3.8 per cent).

You wouldn't guess those kinds of results based on the unexamined rhetoric of western alienation that generally passes for political commentary. But, that public opinion is there, and it won't go away. Ordinary voters are perfectly capable of slamming the federal government for what they consider to be dumb or discriminatory actions. But, they aren't constitutional ideologues.

In the same way that cities have become more and more important in Alberta, the federal presence also began expanding in the 1990s. Edmonton, the city hardest hit by provincial spending cuts in the mid-1990s, got its first boost in years with the expansion of a major army base at the city's north end. Federal agreement on generous tax provisions also helped spark the multibillion-dollar rush to build new oil sands projects. Both incentives featured the work of Edmonton MP and Liberal cabinet minister Anne McLellan. Her personal appeal grew so strong that in the 2004 election she won public endorsements from some provincial Conservatives, including former cabinet minister Dennis Anderson, Edmonton member of the legislature Tom Lukaszuk, and veteran regional party executive Ken Chapman.

Ottawa was putting money into municipal and rural infrastructure across the country. It was putting $3.5 billion over several years into affordable housing initiatives. The Calgary-based energy executives who worried about the Kyoto accord on greenhouse gases had much better access to federal politicians in the early 2000s than they did during the energy policy crisis twenty years before. Beef producers damaged by trade bans related to mad cow disease received a commitment of $680 million from Ottawa, or $80 per animal.

The federal presence spread into the research community, as well. Two scientists at the University of Alberta received a total $18 million in April 2004 from Genome Canada, a federal research funding agency. The university also became the site of the National Institute for Nanotechnology, with the federal and provincial governments each contributing $60 million over five years for its establishment. In 1997, the federal government established the Canada Foundation for Innovation to put money into research infrastructure around the country. By early 2004 it had granted: $154 million to 202 projects in Edmonton; $78.1 million to 132 projects in Calgary; $4.19 million to 13 projects in Lethbridge; $705,000 to 5 projects in Athabasca, site of distance learning university; and, $1.81 million to 4 projects in Olds, site of an agricultural college.

These programs extended federal visibility into the province in ways that straight federal transfer payments could not—even the $3 billion that made up 13 per cent of Alberta government revenues in the 2004–05 budget year. Whatever their effect on public perception, they affected reality for decision makers in the province. Federal participation was crucial to the great oil sands investment boom. Federal-provincial co-operation is increasingly the model for social programs such as housing and for the kind of research-oriented work the Alberta government puts at the centre of its economic development plans. Some of that presence may reflect deliberate federal choices to centralize power, but it is a fact that politicians and voters have to deal with.

Ordinary Alberta voters have never been eager to trust one group of politicians anyway. Alberta harbours an inherent distrust of the political establishment. This strain of restlessness never goes away. Bruce Stubbs, at the time the interim leader of the Alberta First party, which described itself as growing out of the Western Canada Concept and Social Credit, told one audience in late 2003 that the provincial government had grown too close to commercial interests. "Klein has become removed from the people of Alberta," he said. He urged the recognition of rural Alberta as a distinct entity, one whose problems should not be solved merely by throwing dollars at them: "Rural MLAs should not be run over by big-city politicians."

His party also stood for free votes in the legislature, the right of voters to recall members of the legislature, and the right of voters to propose legislation directly through citizens' initiatives. Klein and his cabinet ministers bowed to this populist strain but never acted on it.

Cracked Mirror

The sinuous byways of Alberta political thought rarely get much genuine exploration. It is rarer still to see them explained to the rest of the country, or to Alberta, for that matter. If you see a news story, a book or other commentary about Alberta politics the chances are high that it will feature either the "maverick" theme or "western alienation."

Some of this tendency represents the mental habits of the national media. Their business stories usually have to stick to a factual base. Beyond that, the national media tend to group people in Alberta and on the Prairies as a whole into recognizable and repeatedly used categories: cute, angry, or trying to survive on the farm. The tendency affects local media as well. One of the first stories that CBC Edmonton ran on the federal election in 2004 saw Deputy Prime Minister Anne McLellan interviewed on the theme of western alienation.

Playing to the crowd can help keep viewers and readers. Some of the audience will always lap up regional anger. News organizations also suffer a tendency to reach up and pull a stock story off the shelf. Stock story outlines are attractive. The readers don't get surprised. The editors can run something they feel comfortable with because it's familiar. Better yet, if you write that stuff you can sound like an expert. It's the same internal dynamic that leads to hundreds of clueless stories about "baby boomers"—nearly all of them throwaway pieces masquerading as deep business analysis or clever sociology.

The notion of "western alienation" stems from some genuine sources and is not to be dismissed. But, much of what's written about it and about Alberta doesn't stand up to serious scrutiny. Reading these stories is a lot like watching a low-grade situation comedy.

Here's a sample of what you're likely to see, drawn from a *Globe and Mail* story on January 24, 2004, describing Belinda Stronach's visit to Calgary during the leadership election for the new Conservative Party of Canada: "Belinda Stronach hit the notes Westerners like to hear yesterday—elect the Senate, scrap the gun registry, cut taxes—and tapped into the anybody-but-Stephen-Harper-as-leader sentiment that is growing within the new federal Conservative party. 'I like the fact that she's willing to give western Canada a shot,' said entrepreneur Ryan Loyva of Calgary-based Power Web Solutions Inc. 'A lot of the government out of Ontario and the East gets their word and nobody listens to the West.'"

The assessment of Harper's chances turned out to be obviously wrong. Less obvious was the reinforcement of a clutch of stereotypes that make for easy writing but poor description. There was the standard implication that everyone in Alberta thinks alike ("the notes Westerners like to hear"). There was the Calgary "entrepreneur" as symbol of the region. There was the implication that western Canada had never been heard in Ottawa—despite Joe Clark's election as prime minister in 1979, Brian Mulroney's championing of a free-trade agenda prominently pushed by Alberta, Vegreville MP Don Mazankowski's ascent to deputy prime minister in the Mulroney government, and the existing influence of Anne McLellan, also bearing the title of deputy prime minister.

There was the presentation of Senate elections, an end to the gun registry, and tax cuts as the sum of Alberta's political interests—all of them subject to argument. Senate reform typically brought a response when politicians raised it but never showed up in polls or meetings as a top-of-mind issue that many voters raised spontaneously. The gun registry was a key sore point, but even a number of

Alberta politicians did not oppose a registry for handguns, and the expanded registry had begun with significant support in Alberta cities.

Tax cuts? Opposition to taxes had been key to Klein's election as Conservative leader in 1992 and his subsequent election wins. But, his government had been slipping increases in medicare premiums, service fees, and education property taxes into recent budgets with little apparent protest. Polls had been finding significant support for higher property taxes to help municipalities cope with their budget squeeze. The Canada West Foundation, in a major survey of attitudes across the West in 2004, found that reducing taxes did not rate in the top ten of thirteen suggested priority items across the West taken as a whole. Even in Alberta, tax reduction rated only tenth, with 40.9 per cent of people saying it should be a high priority. That compared with 66.9 per cent focusing on reduced poverty, 67 per cent on improving education, 67.4 per cent on protecting the environment, and 70.5 per cent on improving health care.

The story about the Calgary speech sounded plausible because it repeated so much of what everyone had heard before. But it recounted a list of priorities favoured by Belinda Stronach and a certain audience, not a list that ordinary Alberta voters would have generated by themselves.

The urge to take a ready-made perception off the shelf and make the story fit crops up so often that it overpowers even the most visible facts on the ground. That's what happened with Stockwell Day, whose turn as Alliance party leader depended heavily on a media image that was quickly revealed as hollow. Day's disappointing career as leader featured a lot of wilful blindness by people who should have known better, like quickie biographer Clare Hoy. It demonstrated the ease with which reputations could be inflated in the closed political hothouse of Alberta.

The same surrender to preconception happened after a demonstration in Edmonton on March 22, 2003, against the impending war in Iraq. It was an awfully big event to write off, but the country's media managed to do the job. How and why that happened says a lot about the picture usually drawn of Alberta.

The numbers were slippery, of course. Several thousand people gathered downtown and marched to the legislature. There the crowd swelled. Estimates ranged from about 12,000 to 18,000. Even a number toward the bottom of the range translated into two important facts. The March 22 antiwar rally produced by far the second-highest turnout in a day of demonstrations across the country.

It was triple or quadruple the size of rallies held in Toronto and Ottawa. And in raw numbers, it was likely the largest public rally ever held in Alberta. It may have been twice as big as the next largest demonstration ever held. As a percentage of the population, some Social Credit election rallies in the 1930s may have been larger. But, no public issue in memory had drawn more people to one spot to express their opinion.

How then to explain why the Edmonton rally became an afterthought in national news coverage, when it was credited at all? The usual treatment was to begin the story in Montreal and Toronto, add some mention of Ottawa, Halifax, and Winnipeg, and then say there had also been some protests out west. Neglect was the better of the options. A Canadian Press wire service story that night managed to interpret the Edmonton rally as evidence of a national split between general antiwar feeling in the East and some pro-war feeling in the West.

More than one poll found that Alberta in fact leaned more than the other provinces toward participating in the US attack in Iraq. A year later, people surveyed in the province were still likely to think that invading Iraq was the right thing to do. But, a JMCK Communications poll had found antiwar sentiment was significant in Edmonton and in fact the majority view in that city. Calgary and rural Alberta—not Alberta as a whole—were the real exceptions in national opinion. And, Alberta as a whole was not isolated; it was at one end of a spectrum of split national opinion. Yet, Alberta was generally represented in the media as a place with no antiwar opinion, completely at odds with the rest of the country. Coverage of the March 22 rally reflected that view.

Media organizations and politicians know the script so well that they end up trying to tell the old story even when a new one is unfolding before their eyes. A story in the *Calgary Herald* on the March 22 weekend said a poll done for Global Television had found only 22.7 per cent of western Canadians supporting a US-led war in Iraq. The numbers may or may not have been accurate; it was one poll. Astonishingly, the story went on to claim this weak result showed public resonance with Premier Ralph Klein's support for the war.

Klein himself ran into problems with this tendency to believe stereotypes. He intended to bring a resolution supporting the war into the Alberta legislature. He had to scale that back significantly and settle for a softly worded ministerial statement when he ran into opposition inside his own Progressive Conservative caucus.

These contrary indications—poll findings and Klein's setback with his own party—never achieved national prominence. They tended to pass into oblivion quickly inside Alberta as well. This was not the first or last time something similar had happened. Inside Alberta, the myth of monolithic public opinion serves many interests well.

The Curious Case of the Senate

One classic case in the manipulation of Alberta's image is the call for Senate reform.

The modern call for Senate reform began with the Triple-E (elected, equal, effective) agitation of the mid-1980s. It became meaningful when Premier Don Getty took it on as a personal challenge early in 1987. His first main effort produced an election in 1989 for a Senate vacancy. The election profoundly displeased Prime Minister Brian Mulroney and members of his government. They were even more displeased when Stan Waters, a Reform party candidate, won.

Waters eventually was appointed to the Senate after Mulroney made a point of asserting his independence by waiting for some months. Developments stalled with the collapse of the Meech Lake Accord on constitutional change. The next round of constitutional talks produced the Charlottetown Accord. It was a triumph of sorts for Getty. He did not get clear language about a Triple-E Senate into the agreement, but he did win a commitment to Senate reform as a major nod to the aspirations of Alberta and western Canada. Local critics began saying it wasn't enough; they didn't like other aspects of the accord anyway. One of the major voices speaking against the accord was Reform Leader Preston Manning. A national referendum saw Alberta and nearly every other province vote against the accord.

Getty had gone to extreme lengths in an effort to get Mulroney and Quebec Premier Robert Bourassa to sign on to the idea of Senate reform. It was the best chance Alberta had ever had to remake the Senate as an elected body. Yet, whenever Senate reform came up in future years, there was never much acknowledgement that Manning, an Alberta politician and son of an Alberta premier, had played a key role in blocking a constitutional agreement that included Senate reform, as hazily defined as it may have been.

Klein subsequently agreed to another "Senate selection" in 1998 but acted without real enthusiasm. The Senate project stalled for years. Getty's role in its development turned into a case study of how Alberta can turn on its own politicians as soon as they try to step outside provincial boundaries. During his days as Peter Lougheed's energy minister and minister of intergovernmental affairs in the 1970s, Getty saw himself dealing with a federal government used to thinking of the provinces as junior partners in Confederation. That produced the same kind of disillusionment that affected western Liberals like former Edmonton MP Hu Harries. But, when Getty finally overcame long odds to achieve a major institutional change, he thought could help change perceptions and power relationships, other Alberta politicians and Alberta voters helped block the plan.

A number of polls found plenty of sympathy in other provinces for the idea of electing senators rather than continuing to have the prime minister appoint them. The question was how high anything related to constitutional change was on anybody's agenda. It was not high at all, even in Alberta. Senate reform is needed but not urgently; the country gets along adequately with an unreconstructed Senate. There is no reason to think that a different Senate would necessarily tilt federal decision making toward a regional rather than a party basis. And, as has surely occurred to many Alberta voters, why would you try to solve political problems by electing more politicians?

The link between Senate reform and western alienation keeps getting made, though. It's a surprisingly easy sell. Western alienation and all its by-products get preferential play in the national media because the national media start with the assumption that alienation is what the West is all about. Westerners who talk the loudest about alienation start out with a free pass on their credibility. The more they talk about alienation, the more it is assumed that alienation must be the sole mode of political thought in the West. The more that alienation defines the West, the more it is assumed the people warning about it must be the ones most in touch and most worth listening to.

The closed loop never leaves room for questions such as why *Alberta Report*, the newsmagazine that stood for many years as the journalistic embodiment of western alienation, had to undergo a number of financial bailouts and eventually went out of business for lack of ability to expand its readership, even in Alberta.

Professional Westerners

At the start of 2004, Canada had a new political party with a leader from Calgary. And the Calgary-based Canada West Foundation had a problem. "Despite strong pro-western elements in the new Conservative party, it is not clear what stance its new leader will take toward western discontent," the foundation said in a report written by Roger Gibbins, its chief executive officer, and Rob Roach, one its senior policy analysts.

Westerners don't just feel like outsiders, the CWF report said. "They are outsiders."

In a province that regularly destroys the political careers of Alberta politicians who become Ottawa insiders, that may be a logical conclusion. It may also be logical to conclude that the people most vividly left feeling like "outsiders" are those in Alberta who do not feel represented by the public voices devoted to perpetual anger.

The Canada West Foundation's regular survey of regional discontent that winter had found that people under age thirty were not expressing much unhappiness. The stereotyped expectations built into media coverage showed up in the Canadian Press report on this finding: it referred to the lack of anger among under-thirties as an "apparent quirk" in the survey results. A CWF research director tried to explain the anomaly by saying it could have resulted from young people's general disengagement with politics.

Other explanations seemed ripe for the picking. It was possible that members of a fresh generation were confident about their place in life and uninterested in pursuing the politics of futility. But, that went against what had become built-in expectations. Nor would such an explanation hold much interest for a class of media personalities and politicians who had carved a comfortable niche for themselves by becoming professional westerners. There was always a market and a platform for anyone who could explain why Alberta was unhappy. It was a phenomenon of inertia.

What if regionalism becomes less important to ordinary folks in Alberta than more clearly targeted issues such as taking better care of the environment?

That's one of the problems with "western alienation." It is an emotional state, with no clear objective. How could it have a clear objective? Western alienation is usually linked with issues like Senate reform. A Canada West Foundation poll in January 2004 found that 72 per cent of Ontario residents favoured an elected and equal Senate—a result within a few percentage points of the finding in the western provinces. When Alberta and Ontario both want the same thing, how can that be a top-shelf western issue? But, evaporating issues are not an insurmountable problem. Something else will come up. Trying to end "western alienation" is like the struggle to control people's weight or build up personal retirement funds. If you are in the business of selling diets or financial advice there is no reason for the struggle ever to go away.

The most important thing about alienation in the West is that it is not solely regional. It is not necessarily a condition in which people who live in the West or in Alberta find themselves alienated from the rest of Canada. It is a condition in which shifting groups of people find themselves alienated from their close neighbours, or from their provincial government, or from modern life and a globalized economy.

Regionalism does exist. It is often a reflection of the resentment that people feel when they believe they are not being heard. Former Saskatchewan premier Allan Blakeney once said, while talking about western alienation, that people sometimes have to be allowed to get their way even if they aren't necessarily right; the important thing is to make them feel they count for something. In the West, this feeling of not being heard or counted stretches back more than a century. Some old splits have lingered longer than the legacy of the 1980 National Energy Program. Agricultural discontent stems from a legacy now more than a century old. The Liberal party's problems in western Canada began with the internal party division over the "conscription crisis" of 1917. And, western provinces have been marginally more attracted to various forms of what is described as populism.

Something strange happened to "western alienation" in the last several years, though. It began more and more to be used as a cover for agendas that had nothing to do with regionalism. And, it got twisted around from populism to a front for political actors pursuing their own interests.

A symbolic figure like Deb Grey, the Reform party's first elected Member of Parliament, faced criticism from constituents in her Edmonton-North riding for deciding to sign up for the parliamentary pension plan that Reform had gleefully attacked in the mid-1990s. Their anger expressed a different kind of alienation. It was alienation from politics. Only the politicians seemed immune from this kind of alienation. After retiring as an MP, Grey became an Ottawa lobbyist.

Firewall—No Bricks and No Fire

The original "firewall" letter was sent to Premier Ralph Klein on January 27, 2001. It proposed what the authors called "an Alberta agenda" built on exercising provincial powers in new areas.

The "firewall" prescription: create a separate Alberta pension plan; create a separate Alberta income-tax collection system; create a separate Alberta police force; assert provincial control over health care; hold a referendum to force the other provinces and Ottawa to consider changing the Constitution to adopt a Triple-E Senate.

No public discussion preceded the letter. It was signed by academics and insiders: Stephen Harper, then president of the National Citizens' Coalition (which never held public meetings and never revealed its sources of funding); Tom Flanagan, a political science professor in Calgary and former director of research for the Reform party; Ted Morton, a political science professor in Calgary; Rainer Knopff, yet another professor of political science in Calgary; Andrew Crooks, chairman of the nominally non-partisan Canadian Taxpayers Federation; and Ken Boessenkool, an economist who had served as a policy adviser to Stockwell Day while Day was Alberta's provincial treasurer. Others were rumoured to have taken part in discussions but did not step forward in public.

If this was grassroots action, it was the grassroots of frustrated academics in a mid-level Canadian university and disappointed backroom partisans.

The "Alberta agenda" fell short on technical grounds. The University of Alberta's Institute for Public Economics had held a major conference on the idea of a provincial pension plan in January 1999. Experts from around the country warned that backing out of Alberta's $50 billion in commitments under the Canada Pension Plan would expose the province to enormous risks—high administrative costs, and the possibility that changes in the makeup of the population could leave the province worse off. Individuals' contribution rates could increase, warned Herb Emery and Ken McKenzie, economists at the University of Calgary. The only enthusiasm came from William Robson, a policy analyst at the C. D. Howe Institute in Ottawa. He liked the idea because he saw an Alberta plan as a lever to move pensions across the country onto a different basis. He wanted a shift from a government plan to individual retirement accounts and "a shift to some other tax base."

So, there were huge technical problems. There was also no sign of huge public demand for a separate pension plan or for much else in the firewall proposal. However, by late 2002, the Kyoto accord was being pictured as another National Energy Program and rumblings of western separatism were in the air. Klein told an interviewer that December, "I was listening to a radio talk show the other day and there was caller after caller saying, 'We should separate. We've had enough.' I understand that frustration, and I feel the same way. But, there's still hope."

In February 2003, his government produced a speech from the throne that complained about attitudes in Ottawa and said, "Alberta's ability to be a partner in Canada is compromised by the current federal government, which does not listen to the people of this province." Government MLAs thumped their desks. Public response was split. The national media reacted to a perceived hint at separatism. Klein denied any such leanings and said separatism should be fought. The message remained unclear in March, when a faction at a provincial Conservative convention once again made loud noises about separatism. There was also subtle political pressure. Ted Morton announced he planned to run for a provincial Conservative nomination. Environment Minister Lorne Taylor, widely seen as one of the leading rural voices in the cabinet, was leaning toward the separatist talk. Klein's alternative plan was to find ways to "strengthen" Confederation. In the fall, he announced what became known as the "firewall" committee.

The committee toured from January to March 2004. By any reasonable measure, the exercise was a flop. The lack of interest should have indicated severe holes in the standard picture of an inconsolable province rubbing the scars of its own discontents. Instead, the hearings themselves attracted little media coverage. When Alberta did not act according to its own myths, the media did not pay attention. Failing to note what was really going on made it easier for Harper, by then the Conservative party leader, to continue his support for the "firewall" in the 2004 federal election campaign, as if he were speaking for Alberta and everyone in the province.

An initial committee hearing in the foothills town of Hinton attracted some complaints about the federal government. It also featured a handful of complaints about the Alberta government, which would be a sporadic feature of proceedings for the next two months.

Over time, it became clear that many of the anti-federal messages were coming from members of two little-known groups, the Alberta Residents League and the Citizens' Centre for Freedom and Democracy, which had put $16,000 into radio ads urging listeners to attend the hearings. There was a fair turnout in Red Deer. In Fort McMurray, four people showed up. They proposed a trade mission to show off Alberta to the rest of Canada and expressed lukewarm opinions about the "firewall" ideas.

In Grande Prairie, about fifteen people showed up and told the MLAs to get cracking on what they said were Alberta's real problems: a need to create a proportional representation system of voting and a need to improve trade arrangements with the United States. "Why would Albertans support a regionally based provincial pension plan?" local resident Norm Dyck asked. "Don't drag out gun control, pension plans, and policing alternatives. Albertans know what the real issues are."

Municipal leaders used the meetings to ask for stable funding and more help with infrastructure. Al Hyland, mayor of the southern town of Bow Island and a former Conservative member of the legislature, said, "If you expect the feds to treat you with respect in your negotiations, treat those that are in partnership with you with respect in your negotiations with them." In Edmonton, the committee heard partial support for some of the proposals. It also heard admonitions like one from local resident Noel Somerville: "At present, many of us view the federal government as a much needed bulwark against the ideological excesses of the provincial government."

If there were any hornet's nest to stir up here, the Alberta government was as likely to get stung as anyone in Ottawa. More notable was the public reaction against the renewed anti-Ottawa friction among some prominent Conservatives. After the uproar over the 2003 speech from the throne, former premier Peter Lougheed told a convention of corporate lawyers in Calgary that federalism was working, adding, "But I believe that it's very important that we champion federalism and make it work better. It's time for Canadians to drop their regionalism."

Jim Dinning, widely regarded as Klein's heir apparent, told the "firewall" committee that Alberta should focus on positive solutions to any problems: "Our role in Canada is neither strengthened nor improved by talk of separatism or building walls. In fact, it makes us look defensive."

The committee's final report rejected the "firewall" idea and was inconsequential. Yet, its creation had initially caused a major stir.

What can someone trying to figure out Alberta conclude from all this? A lot of deliberate rattling of chains was going on. The people purportedly thinking about separatism occasionally made it plain they were reviving the tactic that had been on the minds of many Western Canada Concept members in 1982—adopt Quebec's perceived use of threats to get a better deal from the federal government.

But, why was the premier of Alberta willing to go along? He never liked separatist talk, and he was not all that enthusiastic about the "firewall" either. The implied threat may have had some use in his fights with the federal government over health and environmental policy. Klein also had a naturally cranky personality and never minded getting into scraps with people, especially when he felt his pride was at stake. There was more going on, though. The public lining up of figures like Lougheed and Dinning on one side, and Taylor and Morton on the other, underlined the coalition nature of Klein's party, which was still named Progressive Conservative after the federal Progressive Conservative party had disappeared. The provincial party under Klein comprised federal Progressive Conservatives and federal Reform/Alliance members. One of his big achievements had been to bridge the gap between them.

The potential for fracture had threatened since the founding of the Reform party in 1987. Reform began as a curious amalgam of aging, long-time outsiders. Anyone who went to party meetings in the 1980s would have seen surviving remnants of the old Alberta and British Columbia Social Credit parties, a healthy scattering of former military personnel, and, especially from southern Alberta and the Okanagan valley, evangelical Christians. Part of the mindset at work in both religion and politics in Alberta was acceptance that not everyone could belong. Belonging to a minority community seemed inevitable. People in such communities wanted to be "in." But, they did not have an instinct for belonging to wider communities. They wanted not membership, but control. They wanted control because they demanded purity.

Alberta is a province cracked along political and social fault lines. It looks like a monolith only when writers and politicians work to persuade people inside and outside the province that this image is real.

The federal Alliance party's experiment with former Alberta cabinet minister Stockwell Day as leader looked superficially like an Alberta challenge to the rest of the country. In part it was. But, the secret weakness beneath Day's leadership was the rarely admitted fact that he would have had a lot of trouble winning the leadership of the provincial Progressive Conservative party. He would have been unacceptable to half the provincial PC amalgam. Before the Alliance leadership campaign, he had never had to run in an election in which he needed more than 5,000 votes on the north side of Red Deer. Day's move to the Okanagan after he won the federal Alliance leadership reflected the shakiness of his support in Alberta.

One of the results of fixating on western alienation has been to avoid looking at the political conflicts between Albertans.

Preston Manning won the Reform party leadership in Winnipeg in 1987 at a convention where he told delegates their movement was part of a legacy of populist western discontent stretching back to Louis Riel. But before he led Reform, Manning had been agitating for some years for change in the Alberta government. An opening seemed to exist. The newly formed Western Canada Concept party had won a rural by-election just north of Calgary in early 1982; it was blanked out in a general election that fall but still managed to attract about one-eighth of the popular vote. The WCC and similar organizations were generally viewed as voices of regional discontent. In fact, they also represented a reaction in old Social Credit hotbeds against Premier Peter Lougheed's urban-based government.

Manning had no interest in anything associated with separatist rhetoric. But, he saw an opportunity for a populist campaign for smaller government and for the kind of policies that came to be known as social conservatism. By 1983, he was writing and circulating documents that set out his political ideas. Ron Ghitter, a former Conservative member of the legislature, sent one of them to Lougheed on December 20, 1983, and warned in his accompanying letter: "With my rather suspicious outlook on such documentation, it could be a naïve attempt to create a springboard for another political movement in the province."

Manning's biggest effort took place early in 1984. He gathered about 150 people into the kind of grassroots consultation groups that were later featured in the early days of the Reform party, then held a workshop for another thrity-five on March 10, 1984. Some of the results showed up in a document distributed to hotel rooms at the provincial Progressive Conservative convention that spring and in advice sent directly to the government. In a pamphlet from a fleeting entity called the Ad Hoc Committee on Government Revenues and Spending. Manning suggested a one-year experiment with "citizens' advisory groups" created to comment on government revenues and spending. Economies would begin at the top and work down. There would be a full investigation of the government's policy of decentralizing services and offices around the province. Civil servants would receive incentives to improve productivity of programs. This sketchily foreshadowed some of the approach taken by Ralph Klein's first government a decade later.

At the time, Manning was rebuffed. Three years later, he had shifted his attention to federal politics. The switch obscured the central lesson of his tentative forays in the early 1980s: his ideas and those of his supporters were not essentially a regional reaction against federal policies; they constituted policy choices that could and eventually did lead to political battles inside Alberta.

Klein campaigned for a number of years to "unite the right." The strategy was directed at federal politics, but he wasn't thinking just about gaining a stronger federal party. He was constantly trying to cope with the inherent divisions in his provincial party.

While 30 to 40 per cent of Alberta voters generally vote for the Liberals and New Democrats, they can be safely set aside because they have difficulty expanding their support.

What can not safely be set aside is any sizable and motivated faction inside the Progressive Conservative party itself. The factions exist. They can fracture party support. It was common starting in the mid-1990s to hear Red Tories or Conservatives from the Lougheed era express unhappiness with either Klein or some of the people around him. What Klein had to do was keep as many people satisfied as possible. Sometimes that meant placating Red Tories. More often, it meant giving the anti-Ottawa faction a lot of air time to keep them onside.

The need to "unite the right" inside Alberta creates several levels of deception. The message in turn is amplified by public intellectuals with an interest in furthering the cause of regionalism, and by media organizations always ready for the latest instalment of "western alienation"—the only story they think Alberta has ever had.

A BETTER FUTURE

Where to next?

It's an unavoidable question. Alberta's 2005 centennial marks an end and a new beginning.

The official ceremony will be celebrated in the context of a symbolic burning of the province's "mortgage," as the government's net debt has come to be known. The announcement was made simply at the 2004 Calgary Stampede with Premier Ralph Klein holding a banner that said Paid In Full. One would not have been surprised to see it done in literal terms—the premier and finance minister setting flame to a piece of paper representing a decade of fear and unacknowledged shame. What would have been left except a few ashes?

The government had been fixated for years on the idea of paying off its debt in time for the province's 100th anniversary. With a little dubious bookkeeping, it managed to say it had done the job.

Ending government debt should represent a huge psychological lift in a province whose belief in itself was shaken in the early 1990s. Yet as achievements go, extinguishing an entry in the account books seems morbidly empty. It is a small achievement in a province flooded with energy revenues. It merely returns Alberta to the point reached in 1985, when accumulated debt had been whittled to about the last $200 million of long-term loans which there was no point in paying off early.

Alberta has reached a political dead end. The fiscal obsession has gone up in smoke. The 2004 federal election represented a final disappointment for the effort to have a self-consciously Alberta-rooted party take over the government of the entire country. Provincial elections have become lopsided displays of power by the governing party. Frustration has been increasingly replaced by apathy.

Even the concept of provinces may have to change. Alberta is a legal jurisdiction. In some respects it functions largely as a device to gather, hold, and redistribute resource revenues. As an anchor of personal identity, a province does not have the enduring sweep and history of the entire country. And, attachment to a province puts up mental boundaries; Canada is a large land in which individuals want to feel free to move around.

Provinces are a nineteenth–century creation that still serve some useful purpose as a manageable platform for delivery of certain public services. They can be counterweights to the federal government and places in which to experiment with different choices in public policy. They can provide a refuge for people who are fed up with policy choices or social outlooks in other provinces, a role Alberta has served for some. In a world where migration is common and the universal motto of how to organize work and civic activity has become "Think globally, act locally," provinces have also become historical clutter.

Organizing public services more around cities might be examined. That's almost the case in the way Alberta organizes its health system and many other services into sub-provincial regions. Former federal cabinet minister Lloyd Axworthy floated another idea in the 1990s—creating agencies with flexible boundaries across or within provinces to perform targeted work. The weakness of the idea of provincehood shows up in the constant blurring of the line between Alberta and the West; the "West" is a more durable identity, if a more variegated one.

Yet, there is some underlying reality of being Albertan that springs from common history and common geography. When people ask who they are, they look to these particularities, to the work of individuals in a certain place and time.

Everything worth remembering that's been created in Alberta has been at the hands of people. And, that can serve as the guide when anyone wonders, "Where to next?"

People Ahead of Government

Alberta has been bamboozled by money and politics. A new Alberta could be built around people instead.

(This requires a huge shift in political culture.) Albertans have left politics to politicians as long as the money kept flowing. They have to become involved again, to take responsibility for public life.

The single-minded ambition that characterized a decade of financial management could be transferred to reducing the province's large school dropout rate and teenage pregnancy rate (both among the highest in Canada), its 40 per cent divorce rate, and its yearly total of nearly 400 road deaths and 25,000 traffic injuries. Some good steps have been taken on these and similar issues in recent years—measures such as tighter controls on beginning drivers and efforts to prevent or ameliorate fetal alcohol syndrome. What's been missing has been the sense that such efforts are more than just another series of government programs, that they make up the essentials of what people working together are trying to accomplish. How much more could be done if public leaders said human goals were at the core of the public agenda? How many more people would make more prudent choices about their personal lives if their political leaders did not celebrate a kind of outlaw image?

The nature of government operations has to change to accommodate a change of focus from the needs of a single dominant party. Partisanship has to be removed from functions such as communications; departmental communications directors, classified as civil servants, currently operate as political aides. The structure of legislative bodies has to become less partisan. Former Reform MP and later Conservative MLA Ian McClelland was surprised, on moving from the House of Commons to the Alberta legislature, to find that Alberta did not have the all-party committees that are a feature of life in the federal Parliament.

The nature of citizenship in Alberta has to change, as well. The province tends to bounce wildly from aggressive individualism to mass conformity. This is a place where populist strains run deep, but where the insulting practice of naming provincial constituencies after dead politicians symbolically tells voters who really runs things.

Transferring control of public money from government to individuals is crucial.

Much of the more than $1 billion in gambling revenues the province collects each year could be distributed by municipalities or community groups. But, that's small potatoes beside a more urgent issue.

The province's storied self-conceptions disappeared when the multibillion-dollar bonanza of natural gas royalties flowed in the early 2000s. Amazingly, almost no one demanded a regular distribution of royalty dividends to individuals. At best there were occasional calls for rebates on utility bills. Individuals and the opposition parties invariably put these as calls on the government to help consumers cope. What a picture—a province supposedly full of proud, independent-minded people going cap in hand to their governors and asking for their own money by saying, "Please, can I have a little help from you in paying my bills?"

When the billions flow, people truly independent of their government would receive their share of the wealth. That share is any money the government does not currently need. The dispersion of Alberta's huge public wealth to families and individuals would also dampen any future calls to have the province share its wealth with other parts of the country. Much of the sharing would go on informally as people move, or invest, outside Alberta. Distributing the money as dividends rather than as tax cuts would leave the province with fiscal flexibility if resource revenues declined.

The government's grasp on energy revenues also leads to misconceptions about the federal equalization program. Alberta voters are often told they supply most of the equalization money for the "have-not provinces." The total equalization payment for fiscal 2004–05 was set at $9.7 billion. Provincial politicians and others claimed that Alberta was providing $9 billion. The only way to arrive at that calculation was to ignore the fact that equalization payments come out of general federal revenues supplied by taxpayers—not provincial governments but individual taxpayers. Alberta residents provide about one-ninth of the country's tax money. They pay federal taxes at the same rate as everyone else. Their share of the equalization bill is just over $1 billion.

Early in 2004, the small, Alberta-based firm JMCK Communications did a poll asking highly misleading questions about equalization. The background script preceding the question cast equalization as a program that had transferred hundreds of billions of dollars from Alberta to Quebec. No other provinces were mentioned. It also had Alberta supplying $9 billion of the payments in 2004. Surprisingly, given the loaded question, only 68.9 per cent of the people surveyed said Alberta was giving too much; 27.7 per cent said the payment was about right. Asked what Alberta residents should pay for equalization each year, a little over one-quarter said nothing. Of the rest, 50.9 per cent said between $1 billion and $5 billion, 18.4 per cent said between $5 billion and $10 billion, and 2.2 per cent, possibly spiteful at the question, said people in Alberta should pay more than $10 billion. The Alberta Residents League, which commissioned the questions, should have been shocked at what these numbers indicated. About 70 per cent of people in Alberta were willing to pay as much or more into equalization than they were already paying.

Practical Solutions

A lot of things in Alberta work well. Some of the good ideas and practices come out of the provincial government. Every session of the legislature sees low-profile but important acts passed to do things like improve consumer protection laws, create a streamlined family court system, and amend safety codes to include barrier-free access for the handicapped. The province in recent years began stepping up its enforcement of environmental and workplace safety laws. Controversies and disasters usually crop up where the government takes on big projects, or where it insists on making decisions based on ideology rather than pragmatism.

However, a lot of public initiatives work well in Alberta because they are handled on a smaller, sub-provincial scale. The Edmonton public school board has created one of the most admired school systems in North America. Calgary has created a light-rail transit system that efficiently moves masses of people to and from its downtown. The Edmonton health region has created both an efficient hospital system and widely admired innovations. Larger towns such as Leduc and Camrose have created showcase small-urban environments with development of both buildings and park space. Brooks answered a low-income housing challenge. Volunteer-based and publicly funded social service organizations provide everything from meals for seniors to help for abused spouses around the province. A lively community life stitches together a complex network of churches, amateur sports leagues, drama groups, and other organizations that help support families against the unrooted aimlessness of much of mass culture.

All these kinds of activities can operate better with provincial support than with provincial control. This is also true for community groups and for large, public institutions such as school boards and regional health authorities.

The Alberta government has been steadily and purposefully accumulating its organizational reach over the last decade. It is time to focus more on smaller centres of activity, as in the Lacombe Housing Initiative. Often, the province could more usefully stick to a role as a provider of money, of professional or governance standards, and of backup knowledge.

Shifting resources and power toward local institutions also means allowing a larger role for cities. In Alberta, that creates pressure for balancing the interests of cities and rural areas. The general pattern is clear: rural areas will have to give up some of their existing political control over cities (control they may not even believe they have); cities will have to accept that rural areas often need special accommodation because of sparse population densities and wildly variable incomes.

Smaller-scale organization goes hand in hand with smaller-scale ambitions. This is a province tempted by grandiosity. The centennial celebration began, for example, with promises that there would not be a repeat of the bizarre seventy-fifth anniversary celebration that saw the government determined to pay for province-wide activities budgeted at $75 million—a million for each year. The initial talk of spending about $30 million ballooned into a centennial celebration of about $235 million and rising, all without public debate or even much public notice.

The big dreams often tend to collapse with a splat while smaller efforts succeed. Hundreds of millions of dollars went into government loans and loan guarantees for untried businesses in the late 1980s. Some of the investment succeeded, but hundreds of millions of dollars were lost. Meanwhile, scores of Calgary professionals laid off from the head offices of energy firms translated their expertise, their network of business associates, and the nest eggs from their savings and severance packages into successful new businesses. Small isn't only beautiful, it is a stage of successful capitalism. It is an equally appropriate scale for successful innovation in public services.

Remembering this has become both difficult and urgent in Alberta. Two crucial events are taking place at once. The natural gas boom that fuelled the province's renewed growth after 1992 has run into the reality of physical limits. Conventional gas production has begun a slow, steady decline and is expected to drop by another 2.5 per cent in 2005. Alberta's energy future lies in the oil sands, coalbed methane, and prospects for environmentally cleaner use of coal. These are all subject to uncertainties.

Meanwhile, the elimination—more or less—of the province's debt frees up perhaps $3 billion a year of revenue (until the next wild swing up or down in energy prices). That's not just a financial windfall. It is the signal for a fight to win a $3 billion prize (or perhaps billions more).

The most easily anticipated pressure will come from an energy industry looking for royalty breaks. Future natural gas exploration will shift toward deeper geologic zones with higher costs. Coalbed methane will likely not be produced as efficiently as shallow natural gas. The oil sands plants have relatively high operating costs compared with conventional oil production.

Other pressure will come from industries eager to have public bodies pay for applied research in energy, and for tax breaks, or for direct aid for development of non-energy industries. That started before the announcement claiming the debt had been paid off. The Energy Department quietly announced a month earlier that it would allow $200 million in royalty deductions over five years to help firms cover new research costs. A long-delayed debate may finally be held on whether to start building up the Heritage Savings Trust Fund again. That debate may include coming to grips with how far Alberta can keep its tax rates below the

Canadian average, without distorting the national economy or the fiscal decisions of other provinces.

Individual interests lead to different directions—efficient public services; a fairly distributed tax load; a direct share of surplus energy revenues. All these imply that individual Alberta voters will have both the opportunity and the willingness to take part in a large political debate. What happens to the money is less important than that citizens see the money as theirs, and see the right to run the debate as theirs.

The freeing of billions in revenue also intensifies the issue of centralized control. Back in the early 1990s, while various doomsayers were warning that international bond traders would foreclose on Canada, an Alberta government economist named Joe Ruggeri was saying that the federal government's longer-term fiscal prospects looked quite strong, and that its debt was manageable and would shrink over time. A decade later, now a university professor in New Brunswick, he was warning that new proposals to step up the rate of federal debt payment amounted to a lever for keeping money out of the hands of the provinces.

Paying off a few billion dollars a year of an already falling debt load would not actually put much of a dent in the overall numbers; an expanding economy reduces the weight of debt far faster. But, tying up the money would act as a powerful lever for what Ruggeri and co-author Tony Myatt termed "fiscal centralization." Ottawa would gain vast new policy room as its budget surpluses expanded rapidly after 2010; the provinces would increasingly struggle to balance their budgets.

Alberta's example of paying down public debt adds legitimacy to decisions that give the federal government more control over public programs. It's difficult to see how the Alberta government or any Alberta politician could argue that the federal government should not do what the provincial government has done. Alberta has been playing the same game of "fiscal centralization" and may be poised to extend it. The province's balanced-budget law is in practice a commitment to plan for budget surpluses forever. That means the government would like perpetually to take in more money than it needs: a guarantee that it can perpetually expand its power.

The record suggests entrenched politicians will want to continue the unspoken policy of centralized control. That will be backed by the government's inexorable urge to exploit technology. One can easily picture a system, for example, in which individuals are expected to take various medical tests or become liable for medical expenses if they do not. It will be up to Albertans to decide whether and how to fight that impulse.

The logical trap here is elegant and pervasive. Alberta's showcase achievement in 2005 is intended to be the burning of the provincial mortgage. That does more than legitimize any federal effort to move in the same direction. It creates political pressure on Ottawa to do the same. Paying down debt and legally requiring balanced budgets becomes an article of what some commentators, during the 2004 federal election, took to calling "western-based conservatism." Yet, federal efforts to match Alberta's fiscal policies will expand the very federal influence that causes habitual railing against Ottawa.

This is another dead end, one linked to the larger problem of Alberta's role in federal politics.

Looking for an Escape Route

The 2004 federal election summarized the consequences of Alberta's peculiar search for identity in the image of the alienated westerner.

Many factors were in play. Not the least was Alberta Premier Ralph Klein's obvious distance from Conservative Leader Stephen Harper. But, those who saw the outcome as evidence of a lopsided regional clash had a problem. If alienation is central to the Alberta identity, how can Alberta politicians realistically hope to run the federal government? If the Conservative party is really the Alberta party—as some tried to picture it—why would large numbers of people in any other province vote for it? You can be alienated, or you can be influential; you can't be both.

This dilemma raises further questions. Many Alberta voters turned to a Reform party led by Preston Manning, then to an Alliance party led by Stockwell Day, and then to a Conservative party led by Stephen Harper. All three leaders came from Alberta. How would the same Alberta voters react to a Conservative party led by a politician from another province, even a western province?

More pointedly, none of the three leaders could credibly have expected to mount a successful campaign to become the Progressive Conservative party leader in Alberta. If any had tried, the likely result would have been the party's fracture. Each had some strengths. Harper has obvious intelligence, sincerity, and political skills. But, all three are polarizing figures in Alberta as well as in Canada. How can Alberta ask the country to elect political leaders who could not likely win an election in Alberta?

Notwithstanding this problem, the days immediately following the election of June 28, 2004, saw a reprise of a standard game. Some interpreted the result as a "betrayal" by Ontario—without explaining how Ontario voters had been morally bound to vote for anyone. Conservatism was branded as a "western" movement—without explaining why there were Conservative votes in all the other provinces, most of which have a rich and long heritage of conservative attitudes and Conservative governments. The Liberal campaign was branded as built on an anti-western strategy—without explaining why a Liberal deputy prime minister was re-elected in Edmonton, or why the Liberal vote was strong in Winnipeg, Vancouver, Regina, and Saskatoon. The Green party vote in the West was largely ignored, and so was the New Democrats' traditional strength in the West. The existence of issues not based on regionalism was forgotten.

Typically, much of this accusatory rhetoric was featured in the national media. Once again, the game involved amplifying a portion of opinion in Calgary and rural Alberta and claiming this was the voice of the West. Once again, the loudest "western" voices equated "western" with Alberta and Alberta with "Conservative." They ignored differences inside Alberta, and the likelihood that western voters running their own affairs are just as likely to elect New Democrat governments in three of the four western provinces as they are to elect Conservatives (when they don't, in fact, vote Liberal). They ignored the fact that many Alberta voters feel alienated from their provincial government.

These are failures in logic. They make up an extreme case of people hitting themselves on the head in the belief that doing so will make them feel good. It's better to take pragmatic steps toward concrete reforms.

The most appealing is the adoption of some form of proportional representation in voting. Canada is one of the last places in the developed world not to adopt a voting system that allocates legislature seats more closely in line with each party's percentage of the popular vote. That observation aside, electoral reform offers the most immediate hope of ending two major problems.

The regionally concentrated results of first-past-the-post voting artificially make it appear that various regions of the country vote almost exclusively for a single party. This image distorts public debate so badly that some means must be found of breaking it down.

And, some means must be found of breaking down single-party dominance in Alberta—not to change the party in government but to change the electoral system. Trading in one dominant party for another would be pointless. No people who think they belong to a geographic, or political, or cultural minority, should have to make themselves willing hostages to a dominant party. No party should ever think it can enter an election with no real prospect of being defeated despite the likelihood that its opponents can capture at least 40 per cent of the popular vote. A system of proportional representation offers the only relief; it is worth trying despite the drawbacks of such voting reform.

For Alberta, there's an additional appeal. Peter McCormick, a University of Lethbridge political scientist writing with Canada West Foundation policy analyst Casey Vander Ploeg, proposed in 2000 that voting reform could be combined with Senate reform. Making the second chamber of Parliament an elected body within a reformed voting system would respond to a standing Alberta call for Senate reform. Much of the rest of the country could be expected to go along; voters in other provinces clearly want an elected Senate. But, if not in combination with Senate reform—if Quebec proves an obstacle or if abolishing the Senate proves more appealing—then voting reform on its own offers the best answer to regionalism.

Alberta should welcome such a change. It would correspond with deep roots in Alberta history. Municipal councils and the provincial legislature were elected for decades in Alberta on the basis of a proportional representation system known as the single transferable vote. For provincial elections the law was in place from 1924 to 1957. The government put an end to it after the 1955 election, when the system resulted in the defeat of a couple of the Social Credit dynasty's candidates in rural constituencies. Manitoba ended a similar voting system in 1957, as well. Given the local history of democratic experiment and the rhetorical claims of provincial boldness in innovation, it's remarkable that Alberta has left the current movement toward voting reform to British Columbia, New Brunswick, and other provinces.

From the viewpoint of power politics, of course, the failure even to debate such ideas inside Alberta is not remarkable at all. Electoral reform would marginally loosen a dominant political machine's grip on power. Alberta has sunk to a point where it can not really help itself. Instead of calling on its own traditions and leading a national debate on voting reform, it will have to be dragged along by others.

That's why the 2004 federal election result was far more positive for Alberta than the professional westerners who decried it would admit, or perhaps even realize.

Voters across the country put enough Conservative MPs into the House of Commons to create a minority government. They punished the kinds of mistakes that Alberta voters barely notice inside provincial politics, and they left the door open to a change of government. Such results are barely imaginable in Alberta. The federal election showed that competitive politics are possible. Sooner or later, Alberta voters may ask why a one-party system is good for Alberta but not good for Canada.

If the province lived up to its rhetoric, the influence might flow the other way. Alberta used to be a site of political experiment. Now it offers merely a bad replay of the institutional revolution that governed Mexico for seventy years. So, reforms will have to move in the other direction. The federal government and other provinces will have to demonstrate what is possible, and wait for Alberta to catch up.

A crucial problem remains. How do residents of a less populous part of the country or province make themselves heard and have some influence? The question becomes particularly urgent when applied to the relatively small number of commercial farmers—not much more than 100,000 in total—who now occupy vast reaches of the Prairies. But, it is equally relevant for individuals and groups who feel they are on the economic or cultural margins of modern society. The usual Alberta answer is: elect members of the governing party. This strategy has been applied to federal politics, too. It has some pragmatic appeal. It can't be a long-run answer. Voters should never feel forced into choosing a candidate for the sake of gaining influence in a government they generally dislike.

The objective fact is that single-party dominance is a problem only in Alberta. Since 1971, Alberta has elected the same party, often by overwhelming numbers. In that time, the federal Liberals have had to accept two minority governments and three election losses. There is no comparison.

For Alberta voters, that makes it tough to follow the practice of electing federal candidates with a view to having a voice at the table. Electing more Liberals would push the country toward single-party domination federally as well as provincially. The alternative for nearly two decades has been to keep voting for a party that defines itself somehow as "western." But, that choice almost inevitably creates a futile quest leading to more frustration.

A reformed voting system may help open a path out of this dead end. Each region of the country would be strongly represented in Parliament by two or more parties. Proportional representation has flaws in whatever form it is practised. Nevertheless, it offers a practical solution to a chronic and serious problem.

Grounded in Reality

One way or another, these observations reflect the need to base political action on everyday realities rather than on myths and cultural memories of grievance.

They also reflect the need for people to understand one another across distance. Few problems are as difficult in human affairs. Trying to explain one region of the country to another requires information and empathy. Local rivalries inside Alberta generate so much heat, and are built on so much lack of understanding of their neighbours' points of view, that it is often a wonder the province can live with itself, let alone with other parts of the country.

The clashes tend to be institutional, however. Most people try to live their lives outside the arena of public rhetoric. When people meet as individuals they usually find they can get along. They inspire creativity and co-operation in one another.

These qualities exist in abundance. Alberta is home to far more than the comparative handful of hard-driving entrepreneurs willing to pioneer new trails— genuinely impressive leaders like Calgary legends Art Smith and Jim Gray. It is home to more than politicians and their hangers-on.

When you walk down a city street in Alberta you don't see business executives or ranchers or bags of cash. You see mothers pushing strollers or teaching older children how to cross the street safely. In the shops clustered in industrial areas you see welders and janitors. You see immigrant cab drivers who, when you talk with them, often turn out to have foreign university degrees. In the smaller towns you see family-run stores and posters for all sorts of local service groups like the Lions Clubs or Meals on Wheels. Further into the country you see big farm operations and big houses, but you also see weathered buildings and machinery and people with faces on which constant worry is tempered by humour.

What you see when you really look is a lot of ordinary people whose main concern is the daily tending of their personal hopes and their families. They deserve a public life that matches their private dreams.

NOTES ON SOURCES

Most of the information in this book comes from public documents or has been published in newspaper accounts, magazines, and books. Quotations from magazines and books have been identified in the text. Most of the newspaper accounts that served as sources for statements in this book can readily be traced by referring to dates and other contextual information. Unless specifically identified, the bulk of these sources are in the *Edmonton Journal*, often in material written by the author of this book. Some information came from reports in the *Calgary Herald*, and one description of polling results from the *Calgary Sun*. Descriptions of some meetings of the "firewall" committee in northern Alberta were taken from the *Fort McMurray Today* and *Grande Prairie Herald-Tribune*. Some information was gathered by the author's personal observation and was either not published, or published in the 1980s, and thus is probably difficult to find without resort to microfilm at small newspapers. Information from personal observation includes interviews in Lacombe for material in Chapter 4, references to Prime Minister Paul Martin's speech in Edmonton in Chapter 4, references to a man in Taber and to a bumper sticker in Chapter 7, and a quotation from a farmer in northern Alberta in Chapter 8.

The Alberta government publishes a wide range of useful public documents. Those used as sources of information have been identified in the text by general title and date. They include annual budget documents, annual reports of the provincial auditor general, reports of the chief electoral officer, Hansard reports of legislature and committee proceedings, and reports from the Alberta Energy and Utilities Board, particularly "Alberta Reserves 2003 and Supply/Demand Outlook." These are available in many public libraries, in the Alberta legislature library, and by linking through the government's Website: gov.ab.ca.

The Canada West Foundation's many useful studies are also generally available in libraries and through its Website at cwf.ca. This book drew particularly on the foundation's annual "Looking West" surveys of public opinion as well as some special-topic studies identified in the text by subject, author, and/or year.

The Public Archives of Alberta hold the office archives of former premiers Peter Lougheed and Don Getty. Dennis Anderson's memo to Getty in June 1991, Steve West's job recommendation, and references to Preston Manning's forays into Alberta politics in 1983–84 can be found in Accessions 92.519 and 95.445. These voluminous records also contain internal office documents which could not be included in the text for reasons of space but which shed light on the tensions between the Alberta government and Prime Minister Brian Mulroney's federal government between 1988 and 1992.

Information about various public opinion polls other than those conducted for the Canada West Foundation were taken in some instances from contemporary newspaper accounts. Most of the relevant other poll information is available on the Websites of Ipsos-Reid, Compas Inc., and JMCK Communications Inc.

Other sources supplied information on particular subjects.

In Chapter 1: The report of the committee to review the structure of securities regulation in Canada, titled "It's Time" and published in 2003 by the Department of Finance. The Kroeger interview was published in the *Edmonton Journal* on December 8, 2003.

In Chapter 2: The Italian novel is Giuseppe di Lampedusa's *The Leopard* (1958). The comments on Steve West in the 1980s came from Don Martin's *King Ralph* (Key Porter, 2002).

In Chapter 3: Income figures come from the 2001 federal census. The Canada West Foundation published three papers on the potential for an Alberta sales tax in 2000 and makes the papers available on its Website (cwf.ca). They are: "A Better Alberta Advantage," by Roger Gibbins; "Replacing the Alberta Personal Income Tax with a Sales Tax," by Kenneth McKenzie; and, "Tax Reform and Economic Growth in Alberta," by Bev Dahlby. Treasury Department working papers on the shift to a flat-rate income tax were supplied to the author in compliance with a request under Alberta's freedom of information law and were described in a column in the *Edmonton Journal* on January 19, 1999 ("Informed Debate Needed on Income Tax," by Mark Lisac, Pg. A12).

In Chapter 4: Information about municipal financing benefited from *Looking for a New Deal*, by Melville McMillan and Paul Boothe, a comprehensive summary presented to Edmonton city council on April 15, 2004. It and various other reports or commentaries on municipal finances are available from the official Websites of the cities of Edmonton and Calgary. The University of Alberta also maintains various official reports on its Website. The TD Bank report is "The Calgary-Edmonton Corridor," by TD

Economics, April 22, 2003. The section on housing in Lacombe includes information from "2004 Housing Needs Assessment," prepared for the Lacombe Community Housing Initiative by Housing Strategies Inc.

In Chapter 5: The letter to the editor about Ralph Klein as a man of the people appeared in the *Edmonton Journal*: "Academics, Media Clueless about Klein," Pg. A18, *Edmonton Journal*, May 22, 2004. "The call to the Western Assembly" was an advertisement published by what was then the Reform Association of Canada, original copy in possession of the author.

In Chapter 7: The Kallen quote comes from the preface of the March 1992 report by the Alberta select special committee on constitutional reform, titled "Alberta in a New Canada: Visions of Unity." The report also spelled out Alberta's preferences for methods of Senate election.

In Chapter 8: There is voluminous literature on different voting systems. One study of particular relevance to Alberta history is "The Single Transferable Vote in Alberta Provincial Elections," by J. Paul Johnston of the University of Alberta (1992, unpublished). *Federal Debt Repayment as an Instrument of Fiscal Centralization*, by Tony Myatt and Joe Ruggeri, 2004, was published by the Caledon Institute for Social Policy on its Website: caledoninst.org.

A full bibliography on Alberta politics and history would take up much space and is available from many other sources. However, among works to note are: David Elliott and Iris Miller, *Bible Bill* (Reidmore Books, 1987); Alvin Finkel, *The Social Credit Phenomenon in Alberta* (University of Toronto Press, 1989); James Gray, *Men Against the Desert* (Western Producer Prairie Books, 1978); David Stewart and Keith Archer, *Quasi-Democracy?: Parties and Leadership in Alberta* (University of British Columbia Press, 2000); Robert Wardhaugh, *Mackenzie King and the Prairie West* (University of Toronto Press, 2000); *The Prairie West*, ed. by R. Douglas Francis and Howard Palmer (Pica Pica Press, a division of University of Alberta Press, 1992); *Writing Off the Rural West*, ed. by Roger Epp and Dave Whitson (University of Alberta Press, 2001).

ACKNOWLEDGEMENTS

This book would not have been possible without the support, generous co-operation, and helpful advice of various people at NeWest Press: editors Douglas Barbour and Michael Penny, general manager Ruth Linka, marketing co-ordinator Rebecca Whitney, and publishing assistant Darcia Dahl. My deepest thanks to them all for their work on a project whose speed significantly strained the usual publishing schedule and for their good humour throughout.

While the contents include some criticism of newspapers and other media, I have relied frequently on the hard work of many reporters who struggle to do an often difficult job on behalf of the public. Reporting on Alberta politics can be a particularly trying task because of the control exercised by political figures and by some of their communications staff.

Various works on western Canada or by western-Canadian writers formed a subtle backdrop to this book without playing a direct role in it. I have long admired the writing of James Gray and Jim Coleman, and came more recently to appreciate the humour and bluntness of Fred Kennedy in his memoir of life in Alberta newspapers.

This book also benefits from my having had the great good fortune to work for and with a string of remarkable journalists in Regina and Edmonton, particularly: the late Scott Schill; Gerry Wade; Bob Knowles; Garry Fairbairn; John Ward, one of the best writers ever to grace Canadian newspapers; and, Graham Trotter, the finest newsman and one of the finest gentlemen I have ever been privileged to meet. Some, perhaps all of them, might disagree with part or all of this work. Its faults have nothing to do with them and neither do the opinions expressed here, which are solely my own. But, this is a better book for my having seen their example and having learned from them.

Everything I do reflects my love for, and love and support from, my wife Ellen, daughter Maren, and son Matt.

MARK LISAC has been a political writer for over two decades. He began covering Alberta politics for the *Canadian Press* in 1979, and from 1987 to 2001 he wrote a political column for the *Edmonton Journal*. His first book, *The Klein Revolution*, was published in 1995. He is a long-time resident of Edmonton.